The Rise and Development of Calvinism

The Rise and Development of Calvinism

A Concise History

EDITED BY

JOHN H. BRATT
Head of the Bible Department
and Professor of Bible, Calvin College

WM. B. EERDMANS PUBLISHING COMPANY
GRAND RAPIDS, MICHIGAN

L. C. catalog card number: 59-8747

Printed in the United States of America

First printing, April 1959

PREFACE

If there is one course at Calvin College that may be designated as strategic and pivotal, I presume it is the course in Calvinism. That is not to minimize any other course in the curriculum — all of them play an important role in our Christian liberal arts structure — but simply to indicate the integrating and organizing principle of the curriculum. True to its name, Calvin College is Calvinistic. It holds without apology the Reformed faith and outlook and finds its basis in the Word of God, so ably expounded by John Calvin.

The course in Calvinism was first introduced at Calvin College in 1926 by Dr. H. Henry Meeter, my predecessor as chairman of the Bible Department. He did yeoman work. He laid the basis for a very fine course and wrote a respectable text that is highly regarded and widely used.[1]

Upon Dr. Meeter's retirement from the staff in 1956 the College decided to make full use of all the resources of the faculty and reshape the course in Calvinism into a course taught by teachers in several related fields. The experiment was successful and the revised course has found permanent status in the curriculum.

This book presents that part of the course which introduces the man Calvin and traces the main stream of Calvinism through the centuries between Calvin's day and ours. It provides student and layman with a convenient summary of a great amount of historical material. The contributors of the several essays which comprise the book hope that this summary will lead the reader to the more authoritative and detailed studies listed at the end of each essay.

My deep appreciation is extended to my colleagues who join me in this effort.

JOHN H. BRATT

1. Reprinted in 1956 by Grand Rapids International Publishers under the title *Basic Ideas of Calvinism.*

CONTRIBUTORS

John H. Bratt

Born in Holland, Michigan. Educated at Calvin College, A. B.; Calvin Seminary, Th. B.; Columbia Seminary, Th. M.; Harvard Divinity School, S. T. M.; Union Theological Seminary, Th. D. Author of New Testament Guide, *Eerdmans,* 1946. *Professor of Bible at Calvin College since* 1946, *head of the department since* 1955.

Charles Miller

Born in Scranton, Pennsylvania. Educated at Wheaton College, B. S.; Northwestern University, Ph. D. Served at University of Beirut, Lebanon, from 1947-1954, *first in the capacity of professor of history and later as dean. Joined the staff at Calvin College in* 1954 *in the department of history.*

Walter Lagerwey

Born in Grand Rapids, Michigan. Educated at Calvin College, A. B.; Columbia University, A. M.; Free University of Amsterdam; University of Michigan, Ph. D. Since 1953 *professor of the Dutch language and literature at Calvin College.*

Earl Strikwerda

Born in Grand Rapids, Michigan. Educated at Calvin College, A. B.; University of Colorado, A. M., Ph. D. Professor of history at Calvin College from 1946 *and head of that department since* 1955.

CONTENTS

DEFINITIONS OF CALVINISM

"The channel in which the Reformation moved so far as it was neither Lutheran nor Anabaptist nor Socinian." — A. Kuyper

The "irreducible and distinctive system of truth embodied in the Reformed standards." — J. H. Gerstner

The "teaching of Calvin in its widest scope." — A. M. Hunter

A "mode of religious thinking." — J. Vander Kroef

"Theism come to its rights, religion at the height of its conception, and evangelicalism in its purest and most stable expression." — B. B. Warfield

"An embodiment of Biblical Christianity as evidenced in a family of confessions written in the light of the exegetical writings of John Calvin, a family of denominations which are in general controlled by laymen or presbyterial in government, [and] a way of life characterized by a strong sense of duty and a high degree of ethical insistence, encouraged traditionally by ecclesiastical oversight and discipline." — E. Strikwerda

"An all comprehensive system of thought . . . which has come down to us from John Calvin . . . [and] a view of life and of the universe as a whole." — H. H. Meeter

"He who believes in God without reserve, and is determined that God shall be God to him, in all his thinking, feeling, willing — in the entire compass of his life activities — intellectual, moral, spiritual — throughout all his individual, social, religious relations — is by the force of the strictest of all logic which presides over the outworking of principles into thought and life, by the very necessity of the case, a Calvinist." — B. B. Warfield

"A form of religion and Church polity [that] is characterized not only by a theology but also by a singular conception of moral life and social conduct." — P. Chiminelli

1

THE LIFE AND WORK OF JOHN CALVIN

It was a generation after Luther and Zwingli that John Calvin appeared upon the historical scene. He was born on July 10, 1509, in the province of Picardy in France. His birthplace was a cathedral town, Noyon, located some 58 miles northeast of Paris, which, being an ecclesiastical center, held some obvious advantages for young aspiring scholars headed for service in the church. Gerard Calvin, the father of John, was ambitious, industrious, and somewhat materialistic. By dint of hard work he had raised himself above the fisherman and cooperage trade level of his ancestry to a multiple "white collar" job. He acquired the positions of secretary to the bishop of Noyon, notary to the chapter of the cathedral, registrar to the city government, solicitor in the ecclesiastical court, and fiscal agent of the county. His wife, born Jeanne Le Franc, was reputedly of the nobility and distinguished by piety and beauty. John, the second of five sons born to Gerard and Jeanne Calvin, profited but little from her maternal nurture, since she suffered an untimely death.

John Calvin received his elementary education in the School of the Capettes, a private boarding school located near Noyon. Here, as well as in later university years, his closest friends and companions were boys of the nobility, sons of the Hangest family, and from them he acquired cultural habits and social refinements which gave him an aristocratic bearing and frame of mind, and which distinguished him from the more uncouth and rough Luther. At the age of 14 he matriculated at the University of Paris in the school of theology. Paris, a rival of the more conservative University of the Sorbonne, was already infiltrated at this time by "liberalism" in the form of Lutheranism (Luther's writings had been extensively circulated and a small coterie of Protestant sympathizers called Fabians, under the leadership of the Pre-Reformer Le Fevre, was in existence) and by Humanism, with its renewal of interest in the classics rather than in cemented scholasticism, and in man as man rather than in man as an object of salvation. Here he added to his circle of intimates Nicholas and Guillaume Cop, sons of an instructor on the medical staff, who leaned strongly towards Reformation teachings, and a distant relative, Pierre Robert Olivétan,[1] competent Hebrew scholar, who was instrumental in leading John Calvin to a direct study of the sacred Scriptures. He resided at the home of Etienne de la Forge, a wealthy and devout Lutheran merchant who distributed gifts among the poor and inserted religious tracts in the packages, provided a haven for persecuted refugees from the Netherlands, and eventually paid with his life for his Reformation convictions. Calvin's most influential professors during his first stay at Paris included the linguist Cordier,[2] who developed his style of writing, taught him effective habits of study, and disseminated Reformation ideas, and the philosopher John Major, a bitter critic of the Reformation movement who acquainted Calvin with the views of Huss, Wycliffe, and Luther as he assailed their teachings.

In 1528 Calvin was awarded the A. B. degree and transferred the scene of his studies to the University of Orleans. Law replaced theology as his major field of interest and it appeared as though he was headed for the tribunal rather than the cathedral. The reason for this shift of vocational objective was apparently a dual one. His father steered him in that direction, so Beza maintains, since wealth and honor were more readily procurable in law than in theology, and young Calvin himself, somewhat disillusioned by this time as he analyzed current Roman Catholic practices in the light of the Scriptures, was not averse to it. At Orleans he studied

1. Olivétan worked as pastor among the Waldensians in Italy from 1532 on.

2. Cordier found refuge at Geneva later on and died there at the ripe age of 86.

under Pierre L'Etoile, a prominent case lawyer and logician who gave scrupulous concern to detail, and under Melchior Wolmar, a proficient Greek scholar with definite Reformation leanings. Calvin shared lodgings with Wolmar and under his tutelage read the New Testament Scriptures thoroughly.

In 1529 Wolmar received and accepted a teaching appointment at the University of Bourges, and since that institution had on its law staff a famous Italian jurist, Andrea Alciati, Calvin decided to pursue his law studies there. In so doing he was leaving the instruction of a lawyer who stressed the detailed and the specific and entering upon the instruction of one who preferred to explore the general basic principles and underlying philosophy of jurisprudence. Both played a significant role in the development of the incipient Reformer. Schaff maintains that "the study of jurisprudence sharpened his judgment, enlarged his knowledge of human nature, and was of great political benefit to him in the organization and administration of the church at Geneva" but it "may also," Schaff suggests, "have increased his legalism and overestimation of logical demonstration."[3]

Three years of study secured for him a licentiate in law but parental pressures having been removed by the death of his father, he followed his own predilections, turned to the study of the classics, and enrolled once again in 1531 at the University of Paris. From this period of study under the Greek instructor Danes and the Hebrew instructor Vatable there issued the first published production from Calvin's pen, *De Clementia.* It was a vigorous defense of the ethical teachings of Seneca and gave ample proof both of Calvin's literary tastes and abilities as well as his high regard for the resident virtues and vestiges of truth in the pagan world.

Calvin's Conversion (1532-33)

The statement is sometimes made that a new convert is "incurably autobiographical." That judgment does not apply to John Calvin. Only two references to his conversion occur in his works; one in his *Reply to Sadoleto* (1539), an argu-

3. Philip Schaff, *History of the Christian Church,* VIII, 306.

mentative piece directed against a Roman Catholic cardinal who sought to win back Geneva to Catholicism, and the other in his *Commentary on the Psalms* (1557). The change from Romanism to Protestantism and from humanism to Christianity, which very likely came to him in the quiet of his study as his convictions solidified, was in essence a change from "papal superstitions to evangelical faith, from mechanical ceremonies to trust and faith, and from scholastic traditionalism to Biblical simplicity."[4] In the sparse allusions to it in his works he terms it a sudden conversion (*subito conversio*), not in the sense of a Damascan road experience but rather in the sense of a climactic fall of a city by final assault after a long siege, and a sovereign act of God. When "I was obstinately addicted to the superstitions of the papacy," so he confesses, then "God subdued and reduced my heart to docility,"[5] and when he was deluded by the errors and human inventions that had invaded Christ's Church, then "Thou didst shine upon me with the brightness of Thy Spirit . . . Thou didst bear the torch of thy Word before me . . . Thou didst arouse my soul."[6]

Conversion did not mean that Calvin made an immediate and decisive break with the Roman Catholic Church. His delay in resigning his benefices is evidence of this fact. To borrow later terminology, he hoped to be a Puritan rather than a Separatist; he was not convinced at the outset that the church was irreformable from within. And so he joined the ardent reforming evangelicals of France, a motley group of cobblers, upholsterers, soldiers, students, professors, lawyers, and others, and began an intensive study of the Bible. He soon became so well versed in it that he became the acknowledged leader of the group. He had arrived at "the certainty that God speaks in the Scriptures, and the recognition that all truth is contained in them, and that therefore their study and their dissemination are the worthiest object of the talents and zeal of a man's whole life."[7]

4. *Ibid.,* 310.
5. Cited by Williston Walker, *John Calvin,* p. 72.
6. Cited by J. McNeill, *The History and Character of Calvinism,* p.116.
7. Walker, *loc. cit.*

In Relative Obscurity

Shortly after the conversion of Calvin, his warm friend Nicholas Cop, who held the chair of philosophy at Paris, was named to the rectorship of the university. In keeping with an ancient custom he delivered an oration on the event of his inaugural. Entitled "Christian Philosophy" and shot through as it was with Erasmian and Lutheran ideas, it contained a fervent plea for reform along Biblical and evangelical paths. Whether Calvin was its ghost writer is very questionable but it certainly embodied his personal convictions and he was immediately suspected of collaboration. Charges of heresy against both Cop and Calvin were pressed by the Parlement and the Sorbonne. This was the first crisis in Calvin's career as a Protestant. His choice was clear. He must either recant and repudiate all connection with Cop and the evangelicals, or cast in his lot with them and suffer the consequences. Sturdy conviction dictated the latter course. And when the king enjoined suppression of the "Lutheran sect," Calvin fled the city, finding refuge at Angouleme, 250 miles distant from Paris, where Margaret, the Queen of Navarre, who was sympathetic to Protestantism, resided. Here he found shelter at the home of Louis du Tillet, the evangelically minded but timid canon of the cathedral, and drew upon the resources of the remarkable du Tillet library. It was here that he held interview with the aged Le Fevre, and although no record of that interesting visit is extant it is quite likely that Calvin was persuaded at this point that further attempts at reform from within were futile and that there remained no other course but a clean break with the Roman Catholic establishment. Thereupon he returned to Noyon, resigned his benefices there on May 4, 1534, and thus severed the last tie with his ancestral church.

It is quite difficult if not impossible to give an accurate itinerary of Calvin at this point. He travelled extensively throughout France using such aliases as Martianus Lucanius and Charles d'Espeville, spent some time with friends at Poitiers, Orleans, and Angouleme, and in the autumn of 1534 was back again in Paris. It was on October 17 of that year that Antoine Marcourt, rabid and rash evangelical, posted placards all over the city denouncing the Mass as a gross distortion of the work of Christ and identifying the Pope and his entourage as the Antichrist. The result was nationwide rigorous persecution. And since the Protestants of Germany, whose aid Francis I coveted in his contest with Charles V, looked askance at these repressive measures, the king of France, in attempting to justify his actions, defamed and blackened their characters, terming them "anarchistic" and "Anabaptistic," busy with the "foulest sedition" and interested in "the overthrow of all things." This precipitated the second crisis in Calvin's career. Such calumnies as these might not go unchallenged. He resented keenly this injustice to himself and to his fellow evangelicals, and from his refuge in Basel he wrote and published his first edition of the *Institutes,* prefacing it with a masterful apology addressed to Francis I. His avowed purpose was to vindicate his fellow believers from false charges and win immunity for them by declaring expressly their system of beliefs, and to induce others to come to their aid.[8]

In March of 1536 the first edition of the *Institutes* came from the Thomas Plater Press in Basel. It "marked its young author as the ablest interpreter of Christian doctrine that the Protestant age had produced"[9] and projected Calvin into international prominence. He became famous overnight. His work was hailed at once as the acknowledged confession and recognized dogmatics of Protestantism, the Reformation counterpart of the *Summa* of Thomas Aquinas. It found ready translators and thus the Calvinistic teachings were disseminated far and wide. It became the standard textbook at Oxford and Cambridge and held that rating for 100 years. As it passed through succeeding editions until the definitive edition of 1559, its substance remained virtually unaltered but it was expanded, elaborated and developed so that the final edition was nearly five times as great in extent as the first.

8. It served other purposes, of course. As an ecumenical instrument it kept the Protestants from splitting up endlessly, and as a catechetical textbook it informed inquirers and trained converts in the Protestant faith.

9. Walker, *op. cit.,* p. 128.

High praise has been accorded the *Institutes.* Warfield classed Calvin as a writer of theological treatises with Thucydides the historian, Plato the philosopher and Shakespeare the dramatist, and J. T. McNeill does not hesitate to say that the *Institutes* "is one of the few books that have profoundly affected the course of history."[10]

Internationally Famous

After the *Institutes* made their appearance on the market Calvin accompanied du Tillet to Italy. There he visited and forged close ties of friendship with another member of the nobility sympathetic to Protestantism, Renée, the Duchess of Ferrara, daughter of Louis XII and cousin to Margaret D'Angouleme. They carried on correspondence in later years. At this point Calvin returned to Paris, a six month amnesty having been granted by the Edict of Coucy to those who had been charged with heresy and had abjured it, to receive his share of the inheritance of the Noyon property. His financial affairs having been arranged, he set out for Protestant Strassburg, intending to pursue the quiet and sequestered life of a scholar. War occasioned a detour and instead of proceeding directly to Strassburg through Lorraine he planned his route through Lyons, Geneva, and Basel. He arrived in Geneva in the latter part of July, 1536, intending to spend the night there at an inn and then proceed on his way. But God had other plans in store for him. Calvin had come to the third crisis in his Protestant career.

A word about the city of Geneva and her history is in order at this point. It came under control of the Holy Roman Empire in 1032 and in 1162 it was placed in charge of a bishop who, as a prince of the Holy Roman Empire, came to be known as "prince-bishop." In 1283 the Count of a neighboring canton, Savoy, seized the castle of the prince-bishop and his *vicedominus* (representative of the bishop in judicial functions). Thus Geneva came under the domination of Savoy, whose counts were made dukes in 1417. Geneva was restive under this domination and a struggle for freedom and liberty ensued. By 1387 the burghers had won for them-

10. McNeill, *op. cit.,* p. 119.

selves the right of general assembly of the citizenry and as time went on they secured more and more privileges. The final stage to free themselves was from 1519 on. That year was their first major uprising against Savoy. In it they had the help of Freiburg, another canton. In 1525, with the aid of the Freiburg-Berne alliance, occurred the second uprising. By 1528 the duke of Savoy had been expelled and in the third uprising in 1530, the initiative being taken by Berne, Geneva was made a protectorate of Berne. In 1536 she released herself from Bernese control. Geneva had at long last attained her independence.

Protestant Reformation ideas had entered this city relatively early. Lutheran writings made their appearance in the early 20's, and in 1522 Francois Lambert delivered a few Lutheran sermons. The city was not yet ripe, however, for evangelicalism. In 1530 Protestant preachers entered the city with Bernese troops and furthered the preparatory process. On October 4, 1532, Guillaume Farel, "the venturesome, big-voiced, red-bearded little evangelist and controversialist"[11] who had been trained by Le Fèvre, made entry and began preaching, but he was soon banished. Shortly thereafter Antoine Froment, Protestant schoolteacher, began his pedagogical labors, and on January 1, 1534, he broadened his sphere of influence by engaging in preaching. Banishment followed but Froment soon returned to the city. Farel also made return at this time, and the Protestant movement gradually gained in strength. On March 1, 1534, Farel acquired the use of a former Franciscan chapel, and on August 8, 1535, he preached the first Protestant sermon in the cathedral of St. Pierre, the scene of Calvin's later labors. On August 10, 1535, the Council of Two Hundred voted the suspension of the Romish Mass, and in November the Protestant Reformation was solemnly ratified by action of the General Assembly, which unanimously voiced its "desire to live in this evangelical law and Word of God, as it has been announced to us, desiring to abandon all masses, images, idols, and all that which may pertain thereto."[12]

11. *Ibid.*, p. 131.
12. Quoted by Walker, *op. cit.*, p. 179.

First Genevan Ministry (1536-1538)

It was at this crucial stage of Genevan history, when confusion obtained and "an architect was needed if a new structure of solidity and strength was to take the place of the old"[10] that Calvin was led providentially to the scene and received his "First Call to Geneva." Farel confronted him with the challenge but Calvin was very reluctant to assume it. He pleaded his youth, his timid nature and his predilection for study. But Farel would take no negative answer. He called down upon Calvin the righteous punishment of God if he placed his own interests before the kingdom of Christ. Later, as he reflected on this crisis in his career, Calvin said:

> Farel kept me at Geneva not so much by advice and entreaty as by a dreadful adjuration as if God had stretched forth His hand upon me from on high to arrest me.[14]

Calvin was appointed "Professor of Sacred Letters" and began his work of lecturing on the Epistles of St. Paul in September of 1536. Whether he was ever ordained is a matter of question but certain it is that not much time elapsed before the city preachers, called the "Venerable Company," acknowledged his leadership and they remained loyal to him throughout his Genevan career.

Calvin and his colleagues proceeded with dispatch to the task of organizing the Protestant church of Geneva. On January 16, 1537, there was submitted to the Little Council of sixty members a document of which Calvin was the chief author, entitled, "Articles Concerning the Organization of the Church and of Worship at Geneva." This set of articles was designed to serve as constitution for the church; it called for such measures as the introduction of congregational psalm singing to replace priestly chanting, and suggested a choir to assist in this service of praise. It recommended frequent celebrations of the Lord's Supper (Calvin preferred it every Sunday but finally consented to its administration once a month by turn in the churches of St. Pierre, Rive, and St. Gervais) and requested a system of discipline whereby the guarding of the Lord's Table and the exercise of excommuni-

13. *Ibid.*, p. 181.
14. *Opera XXXI*, 26, cited by Walker, *op. cit.*, p. 158.

cation be entrusted to elders ("persons of good life and repute among all the faithful"[15]), the government undergirding and supporting all ecclesiastical decisions that might be taken. It provided for religious instruction of the children and adult church members. To further the last named objective Calvin wrote in 1537 a Catechism (abbreviated in 1541 when the first one proved to be too intricately worded and too long) and formulated a Confession of Faith comprising some twenty-one articles, to which all of the inhabitants of Geneva were to pledge their allegiance.

The path of the Reformers was not strewn with roses. In addition to counteracting charges of Arianism pressed by Caroli, a fellow Protestant who later on returned to the Roman Catholic communion, and opposition led by two invading Dutch Anabaptists, Calvin and Farel had to cope with reluctant civil authorities. For although the ruling councils had given formal approval to the Articles of 1537, they held certain reservations. They refused to relinquish the right of excommunication and they hesitated to demand of all Geneva inhabitants compulsory subscription to the Confession. The unrest and tension grew markedly when the Artichauds, a hostile political party, won control of the city. It came to a climax when the government, without consulting with the ministers, proceeded to introduce Bernese ceremonies (the use of the baptismal font, the use of unleavened bread in the Lord's Supper, observance of special days, and the like — practices abandoned in many other Protestant churches) and insisted upon open communion. Calvin, Farel, and their blind associate Corauld refused to acquiesce in what appeared to them to be an encroachment upon the authority of the church and a profanation of the sacraments, and on April 13, 1538, they were commanded to leave the city within three days. Farel returned to Neuchatel to resume his pastorate there, Corauld went to Lausanne, where he passed away shortly, and Calvin found refuge in Basel. The first stay in Geneva was a matter of history.

Once again Calvin faced a crisis in his career. He saw in Basel an excellent retreat in which to pursue his scholarly

15. Quoted by McNeill, *op. cit.*, p. 139.

ways. But God intervened once again. There came to Calvin the urgent call to serve the French-refugee church at Strassburg. Calvin demurred and pleaded to be excused, whereupon Bucer followed the tactics of Farel in 1536, compared him with Jonah the prophet, and threatened him that if he went into seclusion "God will know how to find the rebellious servant."[16] The adjuration had the desired effect, and in September of 1538 he assumed the pastorate at Strassburg.

THE INTERLUDE AT STRASSBURG (1538-1541)

The Reformation had come to Strassburg in southwest Germany as early as 1523 through the efforts of the pioneer Diebold Schwarz, and it had flourished from the outset. Bucer and Capito were mainly responsible for its promotion and organization. The movement had the backing of the statesman Jakob Sturm, who held the post of mayor of the city for many years. Its educational program had been developed by the ecumenically minded pedagogue John Sturm whose *gymnasium,* where he sought to "form men who are pious, learned, and capable of expressing themselves well,"[17] was to serve as model for the Academy to be set up a few years later at Geneva.

In his three year Strassburg ministry Calvin served as professor of theology in the Strassburg *gymnasium,* lecturing in the Holy Scriptures and helping to train candidates for the ministry; as author, writing his *Commentary on the Romans,* his apologetic piece entitled *Reply to Sadoleto,* a cardinal who urged Geneva to return to the Roman Catholic fold, his *Little Treatise on the Holy Supper of our Lord,* and his enlarged edition of the *Institutes of the Christian Religion;* as ecumenicist, attending conferences with Lutherans and Roman Catholics at Frankfort in 1539, at Haganau and Worms in 1540, and at Regensburg in 1541; and as pastor, leading the five hundred members of the French refugee church. It was in this latter capacity that he was able to put into practice his ideals with respect to pastoral counselling, church discipline,

16. *Ibid.,* p. 144.
17. *Ibid.,* p. 146.

"close" communion administered monthly, congregational singing, family visiting, and church liturgy. His form of worship, of which the main source was Bucer's liturgy, included invocation, prayer of confession, declaration of absolution, singing of the Decalogue, prayer of petition, thanksgiving and consecration, exposition of the Word, recitation of the Apostles Creed, and benediction. These elements have become the pattern for the liturgy of the Reformed churches. It was in this pleasant Strassburg interlude that Calvin married Idelette de Bure, widow of a convert from Anabaptism. With her Calvin spent eight happy years, and her death in 1549 caused him profound grief.

As early as February of 1540, little more than a year after his dismissal, the recall of Calvin to Geneva was broached and discussed by the city fathers. Affairs had gone badly after his departure. Anarchy and immorality were rife. The four ministers upon whom devolved the leadership proved to be unable to cope with the situation. Furthermore, the Guillermins, the political party that favored Calvin and Farel, was in the ascendancy. Calvin's reputation had risen perceptibly also with his magnificent *Reply to Sadoleto*, called "the most brilliant popular defense of the Protestant cause that had yet appeared or that the Reformation was to produce."[18] Thus it was that on September 21, 1540, the Little Council voted his recall. On October 19 and 20 of that year the Council of Two Hundred and the General Assembly verified it. Deputations and communications were sent to him urging him to return. Calvin had come to the fifth crisis in his Protestant career. He enjoyed life at Strassburg and his ministry there was highly appreciated. And he was deaf to their pleas at first. Geneva held no attraction for him. He told Viret that it would be preferable to go to the gallows or languish in a dungeon, and admitted, "There is no place under heaven that I am more afraid of."[19] Farel resorted once more to imprecation and adjuration. Finally, impelled by a sense of deep obligation, Calvin responded affirmatively in those words imbedded in the Calvin seal, "When I consider that I am not

18. Walker, *op. cit.*, p. 252.
19. Quoted by McNeill, *op. cit.*, p. 158.

in my own power, I offer my heart a slain victim for a sacrifice to the Lord."[20] On September 13, 1541, he returned to Geneva and was welcomed with an ovation from the citizenry.

Second Genevan Ministry (1541-1564)

Calvin returned to Geneva with certain well-defined aims and objectives. He envisioned a model Christian community based on the Bible and patterned after the early church. It might have been styled a Bibliocracy since the Bible was to be determinative for both Church and State. The Church, comparable to the soul in man, was by nature spiritual and eternal, autonomous in spiritual affairs, and designed to serve as mentor and conscience of the State. The State, comparable to the body of man, was transitory by nature, autonomous in temporal affairs, and designed to "foster and maintain the external worship of God, to defend sound doctrine and the condition of the Church, to adapt our conduct to human society, to form our manners to civil justice, to conciliate us to each other, to cherish common peace and tranquility. . . ."[21]

"Its object is not merely . . . to enable men to breathe, eat, drink, and be warmed . . . but it is, that no idolatry, no blasphemy against the name of God, no calumnies against his truth, nor other offences to religion, break out and be disseminated among the people; that the public quiet be not disturbed, that every man's property be kept secure, that men may carry on innocent commerce with each other, that honesty and modesty be cultivated; in short, that a public form of religion may exist among Christians, and humanity among men."[22]

On the day of his return Calvin proposed to the little Council a reconstitution of the Church, and a committee of six was appointed to assist him in formulating the proposals. The document they framed was called *Ordonnances Ecclesiastiques.* It was modified by both the Little Council and the Council of Two Hundred, and involved several compromises that Cal-

20. *Ibid.,* p. 159.
21. *Inst.* IV, XX, 2.
22. *Ibid.,* 3.

vin had to make. On November 20, 1541, it was adopted by the General Assembly.

The *Ordonnances,* on the basis of the institution of Christ as reflected in the primitive church, provided for four classes of church officers: Pastors (called the Venerable Company), who were to preach the Word, administer the sacraments, admonish the disorderly, participate in the examination of ministerial candidates, exercise discipline with the elders, and meet weekly for discussion of Biblical teachings; Teachers, who were to instruct in the Word and lecture in theology and in the liberal arts; Elders, who were to exercise surveillance over the doctrine and conduct of the church, admonish the erring, rule the church and exercise discipline; and the Deacons, who were to manage the funds and distribute to the needy. Liturgical directions regarding the administration of baptism and the Lord's Supper, conducting funerals and visiting the sick were also included. The main purposes of the *Ordonnances* were "to give a measure of self-government elsewhere unknown in Protestant lands to the Church, while maintaining helpful relations to the State; and to put into operation an effective discipline whereby the Church might fulfill that which Calvin regarded as its most urgent duty, the initiation of its members into, and their maintenance in, right doctrine and right living."[23] McNeill states that "this historic document may justly rank as one of the most important of ecclesiastical constitutions, since in it the principles of later Reformed Church polities found classical expression."[24]

Since the first fourteen years of Calvin's second Genevan ministry were rather stormy and were marked by extensive controversy, it is customary to divide his work into the Period of Struggle and Conflict, and the Period of Triumph.

Period of Struggle and Conflict (1541-1555)

The conflicts and tensions of this period stemmed from various sources. Opposition to Calvin and his reformatory measures was induced by varied, often inter-related reasons.

23. Walker, *op. cit.,* p. 266.
24. *Op. cit.,* pp. 160-161.

There were those in Geneva who had been instrumental in his dismissal in 1538 and who did not favor his recall in 1541, and they joined with others in their disaffection. The city councils, although backing Calvin in the main, were reticent about relinquishing the right of exercising discipline and the prerogative of excommunication. In addition, there were sincere theological differences that precipitated conflict.

Speaking generally, the major group opposed to Calvin and his program was the Libertines. Some of them were descendants of the oldest and most distinguished families of Geneva, who had used the Reformation to achieve independence but who had little love for the Reformation doctrines and who resented the influx of foreigners as well as the fact that the reins of government had fallen into the hands of a Frenchman. Others of them had a theological basis for their resistance to the repressive disciplinary measures. They were antinomian, and "under the pretext of the freedom of Spirit, they advocated the unbridled licence of the flesh."[25] Still others of them chafed under restraints and resented any encroachment upon their personal freedom and pursuit of pleasure. Many of the prohibitive rules and laws had been on the statute books long before Calvin's coming, but they had fallen into desuetude and Geneva had acquired the dubious distinction of being a wild and licentious city.

Cases of discipline involved some elected leaders as well as members of the city's most distinguished families. Among those involved were: Pierre Ameaux, Captain-general of the city and manufacturer of playing cards, who criticized Calvin bitterly when the card manufacturing business deteriorated and when Calvin hesitated to sanction Ameaux's divorce from his philandering wife; Ami Perrin, former member of the Little Council and charter member of the socially elite, whose wife was imprisoned for dancing at a wedding and who thereupon defiantly denounced and heaped abuse upon Calvin; Jean Favre, who made sport of the key question in the marriage form; Berthelier, son of the martyred patriot who helped win freedom from Savoy in 1519, who demanded the privilege of communion despite his notoriously immoral life;

25. Schaff, *op. cit.*, p. 499.

and Jacques Gruet, who was guilty of overt irreligion and blasphemy.

Heretical opponents included Sebastien Castellio, Jerome Bolsec, and Michael Servetus. A ministerial aspirant, Castellio was approved by the Little Council but rejected by Calvin and his colleagues because he regarded the *Song of Solomon* as an uninspired, obscene piece and disagreed with the traditional Reformed interpretation of the clause in the creed, "He descended into hell." Castellio became embittered, denounced Calvin and other ministers, and wrote a work, *Whether Heretics Ought to Be Punished,* which elevated him to the rank of "the most distinguished sixteenth century exponent of religious toleration."[26] Bolsec, former monk, competent physician with deep theological interests, maintained that the doctrine of predestination taught by Calvin (thereby jeopardizing Calvin's reputation as Bible interpreter) made God an arbitrary tyrant. After various debates on the subject Bolsec was banished and the Council gave Calvin a vote of confidence. The celebrated Servetus, likewise a physician with speculative gifts and a resourceful mind, repudiated the doctrine of the Trinity. Having become a marked man on the continent, he was apprehended in Geneva and executed there, dying with the prayer on his lips, "Jesus, Son of the Eternal God, have mercy on me."

The Period of Triumph (1555-1564)

From 1555 on life in Geneva for Calvin took on a much more pleasant and agreeable hue. The Libertine movement had collapsed, with its diehards making their headquarters at Berne; the heretics had either been converted, banished or executed; the consistory had acquired more autonomy in spiritual affairs; the eldership had been broadened in that it now also included members of the Council of Two Hundred; and the city government was giving Calvin without reservation the support he coveted and needed. Another contributing factor to Calvin's augmented popularity was the influx of religious refugees (between 1549 and 1559 some 5017 were given residence in the city), many of whom were admitted to citizenship

26. McNeill, *op. cit.,* p. 169; cf. pp. 176-7.

privileges. By 1558 they were also made eligible for the office of the magistracy.

One of the most notable achievements of this final period was the establishment in 1559 of the Academy of Geneva, with the expert Greek scholar and teacher Beza as the first Rector. When it opened its doors on March 5, 1559, there were 162 students enrolled. By 1565 the student body numbered 1600. There was a cosmopolitan cast to the student body and this seminary of Reformed Protestantism and the entire city as a model Christian Commonwealth was termed by John Knox "the most perfect school of Christ that ever was in the earth since the days of the Apostles."[27] The Academy sent trained leaders to the continent and to the British Isles, all of them imbued with Calvinistic teaching.

In addition to his ordinary labors of preaching on Sunday and every other day of the week, presiding over the consistory and expounding Scripture to the Venerable Company, Calvin lectured on theology in the Academy, his Commentaries being the fruits of such endeavor; arranged and attended colloquies with fellow Protestants, finally uniting with Bullinger and the Zwinglians in the Consensus of Zurich; and continued his writing. His correspondence was voluminous and his *Institutes* underwent further revision in successive editions of which "the apologetic purpose gradually receded and the instructional purpose became dominant."[28] His service to the city as Christian citizen included: sermons on citizenship prior to the city elections; promotion of sanitation measures (as, for example, the inspection of food); agitation for a hospital and poor-house; and encouragement of a cloth and silk industry which brought prosperity to the city of Geneva. After considerable suffering and after a touching farewell with the city fathers, he passed away on May 27, 1564, his departure being deeply mourned by all of Protestantism.

27. Quoted in Schaff, *op. cit.*, p. 1518.
28. E. Harris Harbison, *The Christian Scholar*, p. 151.

BIBLIOGRAPHY

Audin, J. M. V., *John Calvin,* Louisville, Ky., n. d.

Borgeaud, *Histoire de l'Université de Geneva,* 1900.

Breen, Quirinus, *John Calvin, a Study in French Humanism,* Grand Rapids, 1932.

Bungener, L. L. F., *Calvin,* Edinburgh, 1863.

Dakin, Arthur, *Calvinism,* London, 1941.

Doumerge, E., *Jean Calvin: les Hommes et les Chose de son Temps,* Lausanne, 1899-1927.

Dyer, T. H., *The Life of John Calvin,* London, 1850.

Foster, Herbert D., "Geneva before Calvin," in *Collected Papers,* I, New York, 1929.

Harkness, Georgia, *John Calvin, the Man and His Ethics,* New York, 1931.

Hunt, A. H. Carew, *Calvin,* London, 1933.

Hunter, A. Mitchell, *The Teachings of Calvin,* Glasgow, 1950.

Lammertse, J., *Calvijn en Calvinisme,* 's-Hertogenbosch, the Netherlands, 1932.

Mackinnon, J., *Calvin and the Reformation,* London, 1936.

McNeill, John T., *The History and Character of Calvinism,* New York, 1954.

————————, "Thirty Years of Calvin Study," in *Church History,* XVII, 1949. pp. 207-240.

Pauck, Wilhelm, "Calvin and Bucer," in *Journal of Religion,* IX, 1929, pp. 237-256.

Penning, L. *Genius of Geneva,* Grand Rapids, 1954.

Reyburn, Hugh, *John Calvin, His Life, Letters and Work,* London, 1914.

Schaff, Philip, *History of the Christian Church,* VIII, New York, 1910.

Stickelberger, E., *Calvin: A Life,* Richmond, Va., 1954.

Walker, Williston, *John Calvin,* New York, 1906.

Warfield, B. B., *Calvin and Calvinism,* New York, 1931.

Wileman, W., *John Calvin,* London, n. d.

2

THE SPREAD OF CALVINISM IN SWITZERLAND, GERMANY, AND FRANCE

The spread of Calvinism was unusual. Catholicism had been maintained by civil and military force and was throughout Europe an obligation of birth and citizenship. Lutheranism likewise survived and expanded only because it became a religion of politics. Calvinism, in contrast, having in general neither civil nor military authority to support it, had only the appeal of its consistent logic and self-apparent Biblicism to popularize it. Within a generation, on such a basis, Calvinistic ideas had spread across Europe and, even where Reformed churches were not established, Calvinism was to leave its mark. The impact was not personal, as it was with Lutheranism, nor ecclesiastical as with Catholicism; but primarily ideological.

This phenomenal expansion of Calvinism is incomprehensible if, as many consider it today, Calvinism is defined as little more than a narrow, syllogistic, theological system. At times, unfortunately, Calvinism has been little more than this. A scholastic trend, moving in this direction, began to develop about a century after Calvin's death and is best illustrated by the classic "five points," which find their paradigm in TULIP, a summary which stripped Calvin's ideas of their vitality and breadth. Although these doctrines are a logical part of Calvin's thought, his primary emphases are elsewhere and his most revolutionary assumptions elude attention.

For instance, contrary to the contention of most historians, Calvin did not lay unique stress on the doctrine of Predestination. In his day this doctrine was widely accepted in Christendom. Few of his sermons even touched the topic and most of these were preached during the last decade of his long life and then only as the result of his conflict with Bolsec, a member of the Reformed community. Luther at first, sharing with Calvin a respect for Augustinian thought, also accepted Augustine's ideas on Predestination. Even in the Catholic camp, the Spiritual Exercises of Ignatius of Loyola, the founder of the Jesuits, clearly state that "no one can be saved without being predestined and without faith and grace." Only after Calvin's death, when the variation in the meaning of Predestination became apparent, did Predestination become an issue of great and general controversy.

In Calvin's day his most controversial doctrine was not Predestination but his idea that Christ's body is spiritually and really though not physically present in the bread and wine used at the Lord's Supper. Although the doctrine was in all likelihood inspired by the writings of the Englishman John Wycliffe, who had lived a century and a half earlier, its chief advocate during the Reformation was Calvin. On even this issue, however, he was willing to modify his position if the Church of Christ could again be united. Curiously, this doctrine which in his own time was one of the hallmarks of Calvinism, was cautiously neglected by the formulators of the Heidelberg Catechism and was only casually mentioned by those writing the Westminster articles of faith. These two are the greatest creedal statements of Calvinism.

There is perhaps no more dramatic indication that the emphases of Calvinism changed after Calvin's death than the fact that none of the catechisms or confessions of faith he helped write are used today. Calvinism as an historical movement has, in general, preserved the distinctive perspectives of Calvin but it has been dynamic rather than static, led by men who were conscious that a changing world called for changing emphases. It has been Calvinistic — in the spirit of Calvin — rather than Calvinist. Hence, there have been few disciples of Calvin but there have been a host of those who found in his ideas the key to a Biblical Christian faith.

This was, in fact, the role Calvin had cast for himself. He was conscious of living in the sixteenth century and of attempting to establish the essence of first century Christianity in the sixteenth. He worked to redress the wrongs not only of degenerate Catholicism but more particularly of inadequate

Lutheranism and Anabaptism. His major emphases in this program may be summarized under five heads.

First and certainly basic in all of Calvin's thought is a healthy Biblicism, a belief in both the authority and sufficiency of Scripture. The Bible, which shared with Nature the role of revealer of God, was the only acceptable rule of faith and practice. A doctrine or tradition not based on Scripture was no more than a human convenience and was recognized as such. Hence, ancient practices, however fine; pronouncements of ecclesiastical authorities, however wise; or even decisions of Church councils, however universal, were authoritative only in so far as they reflected the clear teaching of Scripture. This position was distinct not only from that of the Roman Catholics, who placed the traditions of the Church Fathers and the pronouncements of ecclesiastical councils on a par with the Bible, but also from the developing Lutheran practice, which considered traditions to be binding if they did not clearly conflict with the teaching of Scripture and which assigned authority to the pronouncements of the theologians and, eventually, of the princes, who sat as virtual bishops. Calvin's position, which was in fact a reaffirmation of that of the thirteenth century Peter Waldo and of John Wycliffe, is basic to all of Calvin's other ideas and accounts for the paramount role of Bible study and exegetical preaching in Calvin's ministry. Both his *Commentaries* on the whole Bible, except for the book of Revelation, and his sermons reflect this effort to know what Scripture says when it is studied intelligently, without the restraint of preconceived theology or tradition. Certainly this Biblicism was particularly important in the historical expansion of Calvinism.

Calvin's second major contribution, the Presbyterian form of church government, was a logical product of his Biblicism. Though conscious that no particular form of church government was commanded by Scripture, Calvin recognized the validity of New Testament practice and saw in it the recognition that the highest church authority was not only collective and representative of the elect but also independent from the State. Hence, while no unique divine authority was given these representative bodies, variously called consistories or presbyteries, as assemblies of the mature spiritual leaders of the local Christian community (elders and ministers) theirs was the responsibility on earth for interpreting Scripture and for exercising Christian discipline. Other Protestant groups had experimented with similar representative organization before Calvin but he developed it most fully. A Calvinist projection from Scripture was the creation of synods or general assemblies which were representative of the consistories and assumed the responsibilities for establishing common Christian agreement and for common programs of action. Calvinist synods were first introduced in the Reformed church of France in its organization of 1559 and differed from the secularly appointed church councils which previously had been called synods. As originally conceived, such Reformed synods were not denominational but rather national assemblies of those willing to accept the authority of Scripture; subsequently they became sectarian. Only the Synod of Dort was in any sense international.

The Calvinist concept of church government contrasted with the Roman Catholic theory that a mystical divine authority was given to the apostles and was passed on by the clergy from generation to generation (Apostolic Succession) and that among the clergy the position of the bishop of Rome, or the Pope, was superior to that of the other clergy. According to this theory the Roman church as an ecclesiastical organization could speak as the authoritative voice of God. (The Doctrine of Papal Infallibility, a somewhat different idea, one which modified the practices of the Roman Catholic Church, was not proclaimed until 1870.) The Reformed position also contrasted with the Lutheran one, which in theory held to the independence of each congregation as a unit of pure democracy but in practice permitted responsibility in matters of discipline, church property, and church appointments to be exercised by the prince who acted as the bishops previously had done. Subsequently even doctrine fell under the control of the prince. Obviously, where the Protestants constituted a minority, neither of these positions was possible and Calvin's was gladly received.

The third contribution of Calvin was his theory of civil society. Sometimes called Bibliocracy, it is a natural corollary of the second. He did not feel that Scripture required any particular form of government — monarchy, aristocracy, or democracy. However, he felt that whatever the form, the State received its authority only from God and had as its primary responsibility the application of the revealed will of God. In his view both the Church and State are subject to a single common authority, the Holy Scriptures, and hence neither is subject to the other. However, it must be remembered that the right to interpret Scripture rested with the consistory which, therefore, outlined the moral role of the State. There was in Calvin's theory no domination of the Church by the State, as in Lutheran practice, nor, as in the Catholic position, did all civil authority rest on a grant of power from the institutionalized Church speaking for God. The Calvinist position, it should be noticed, is also in contrast with the modern idea of a secular state totally divorced not only from the church and religion but also from divine law. Both the natural right and pragmatic theories of democracy, which recognize popular sovereignty and make the question of right a matter of majority vote, are opposed to the position of Calvin.

Calvin's fourth emphasis may well be called Moralism, although he himself would probably protest the choice of the term. True righteousness and godliness was the goal Calvin sought, not formal obedience to a legal code such as is usually associated with Puritanism. For Calvin, godly living marked by a consistently moral conduct was a logical gift to God in thanks for His free salvation. It was the only possible conduct for a man who recognized that, as the result of salvation, his body was no longer his own but God's.

Calvin's emphasis on godly living was a practical attempt to correct a situation he found deplorable. At times, unfortunately, his practice seems to have gone beyond his theory. It appears that the first phases of the Reformation aggravated rather than ameliorated the problem of personal immorality. Although the Lutherans had given the immorality of the Roman clergy as one reason why they should not be respected, Lutheranism was not marked by moral reform or ethical theory. In fact, many of Luther's disciples, particularly among the laity, lived less than exemplary lives and, on one occasion, Luther and his fellow theologians granted, in an effort to moderate his licentiousness, a dispensation to enter a bigamous marriage to Philip of Hesse, the most powerful of the Lutheran princes. In fleeing the formal moralism of the Catholic penitential system, the Lutherans failed to develop an adequate substitute.

The situation Calvin was to find in Geneva was scarcely more admirable. The citizens had become Protestant for the crudest of political reasons, in an effort to retain the aid of Berne against their rightful rulers. It appears that their private morals were as flexible as their public. Farel and the other foreign missionaries sent to Geneva by Protestant Berne, found the ground exceedingly stony and used government authority to enforce private morality. Almost desperate. Farel implored Calvin to remain in Geneva to use his great talents of persuasion there. Understandably, when Calvin found the prevailing lack of morality in the Roman Church also among the followers of Luther and in Geneva, he could scarcely have evaded the responsibility to preach godly living and to develop a Biblical basis for such living. This emphasis has remained a consistent mark of historic Calvinism.

Calvin's final and best known contribution was a system of theology. To designate it as Calvin's theology is both a misnomer historically, because it was fundamentally a restatement of Augustine's, and a violation of all that Calvin was attempting to do, namely to let Scripture speak for itself without the imposition of alien philosophies. Calvin felt that Scripture itself emphasized its own authority, God's sovereignty, salvation by faith, predestination, and the other doctrines usually associated with Calvinism. On these issues Calvin was in substantial agreement with Augustine, as the *Institutes of the Christian Religion* clearly show. His major disagreement with Augustine, the Roman Catholic bishop, was over the authority of the institutionalized Church. The last revision of Calvin's *Institutes* in 1559 provided the first complete and consistent theology of the Reformation and the one which today remains the most influential.

The story of the spread of Calvinism is frequently confusing because groups which accepted any of the various emphases made by Calvin were frequently called Calvinistic. Churches in Germany which before 1536 had experimented with what is now called Presbyterianism were called Calvinistic as were the English Congregationalists who accepted Calvin's theology while rejecting this very view of church government. Lutherans who did little more than reject the doctrine of Consubstantiation were called Calvinists, as were the ardent Reformed of the Netherlands who silently accepted Erastianism. Obviously Calvin had detected many of the major weaknesses of sixteenth-century Christianity and had proposed reasonable solutions to the problems. His solutions were popular. However, because there was no compulsion to accept the whole complex of his ideas, the nature of what was called Calvinism varied considerably from place to place. The future was to be even more confusing. Any group which ever had held to any of the major ideas of Calvin was known as Calvinist, however far it had departed from his basic emphases.

As a second generation reformer, Calvin provided positive solutions to problems which had only been defined by Luther and Zwingli. He had a perspective which only time could give. Although he did not consider it his mission, it would seem that Calvin saved the Reformation from self-destruction.

Calvin's role is more understandable if it is recognized that Luther's reformation was not only incomplete and inconsistent but was only one more in a long series of attempts to reform the Christian Church. The Lutheran movement, which began as a righteous cry against a grossly abused but peripheral doctrine of the Church, the granting of Indulgences, tended to seize upon single issues. Luther himself was so obsessed by the doctrine of Salvation by Faith that many other phases of Christian life suffered total neglect. Paradoxically, even on this pet doctrine Luther failed to break completely with the Romanist tradition. The issue was not, as he recognized, that the Catholic Church insisted that faith was not needed for salvation or that an abundance of good deeds was. Luther's main disagreement with the Catholic tradition concerned the claim of the Roman Church that faith and works were effective for salvation only through the authority of the Church and through the sacraments which it monopolized. Luther, in contrast, insisted that man was saved not by the sacraments nor through the Church but as each man, serving as his own priest, makes peace with God. Luther's position became ambiguous, however, after he developed his own sacramental system because he was to hold in general terms to baptismal regeneration and his doctrine of the Lord's Supper only half abandoned the Catholic position.

Many of the pre-Lutheran reformers were more consistent and more thorough than he in their proposals. They too, however, had failed to find a satisfactory principle of authority to substitute for papal institutionalism on the one hand, and anarchic mysticism, on the other.

As early as the fourth century, when Christianity was recognized as the state religion of the Roman Empire, men had been attempting to purify the Church. For instance, the monastic movement, which received its primary emphasis in Western Europe from Benedict about 520, assumed that the official church with its sacramental system was inadequate and sought godliness by retreat from the world. Early monasticism was fundamentally a lay movement and, without directly challenging the official doctrines of the Church, it bypassed them. The ideals of the Christian life were hard work, austerity, righteousness and communion with God rather than formal religion. This mysticism with its deliberate attempt to reestablish the Christ-disciple relationship did, in fact, establish a parallel practice of salvation which virtually ignored the institutionalized Church. Mystic communion with God and not the sacraments was the way of salvation.

More actively reformist was the movement developed about 1175 by Peter Waldo, a wealthy merchant from Lyons, in Southern France, who abandoned trade to preach salvation. Initially this effort of the better educated townsmen to instruct the peasants and lower classes in the teachings of the Scriptures had the blessing of the Church. Waldo arranged for a translation of the Bible into the vernacular French of the area and launched missionaries on programs of expository preaching. Such a Bible-centered program soon bore fruit, some of which was unacceptable to the Church. Waldo concluded that the Scriptures and not the Church are the primary Christian authority and that the sacraments, though desirable, are not necessary for salvation. Consequently the bishops and finally the pope turned against him. Soon condemnation led to active persecution. The Waldensians along with the Albigensian heretics of the same area were virtually exterminated by a crusade begun in 1208. Scattered Waldensian refugee communities remain until this day in the high Alps of France and Italy, in Switzerland, and even in the United States. Calvin came into contact with one such group shortly after his flight from France and assisted them in a translation of the Bible. He found his own spirit so sympathetic with theirs that he, at one time, called himself a Waldensian.

A more radical reforming movement and one of considerably greater influence and intellectual respectability was that launched in the heart of English Catholicism by John Wycliffe about 1375. During the following generation his ideas were championed by John Huss in Bohemia, the western part of modern Czechoslovakia. Both of these men were university professors and had the support of some of the most prominent nobility. Their views were, however, basically the same as those of the long series of medieval reformers: Scripture was considered the ultimate religious authority, the sacraments were not considered necessary for salvation, the priesthood was criticised as being contrary to the teachings of Jesus, the papacy was condemned as being without any Biblical warrant, and indulgences were castigated as vigorously as they were by Luther more than a century later. In spite of his radical views and the activities of his Lollard missionaries, Wycliffe was able to die a natural death. In large measure this was because he was protected by the most powerful nobleman of England, John of Gaunt, who was using Wycliffe's righteous reputation to gild his own dubious one. Huss, however, was less fortunate. In spite of Emperor Sigismund's "safe conduct," he was tried, condemned as a heretic, and burned at the stake during the Council of Constance in 1415.

All of the reforming movements before Calvin, including many not mentioned, floundered on the critical issue of religious authority. It was a simple matter to deny the right of the Roman Church to speak in the name of God and to assert that Scripture alone constitutes the basis of belief and practice, but the application of these beliefs in a Christian community proved difficult. Some insisting on the right of each individual to interpret Scripture for himself, developed an anarchy, with each man acting as if he were pope. Others permitted this critical function of interpreting Scripture to be exercised by a generally accepted popular leader or by a secular ruler. Neither of these solutions was a logical improvement on the Roman position.

This was the crisis Calvin faced in 1536 when, a young man of 26, he arrived in Geneva as a religious refugee from France. Protestantism had gone to seed. German Lutheranism was splintered by bitter controversy. Furthermore, the Anabaptists had broken from the main stream of Lutheranism and were beset by hyper-literalism, antinomianism, and anarchy. Protestantism in German Switzerland, though not as disorganized as in Germany, was in retreat. The great Swiss humanist, Ulrich Zwingli, had begun the movement in 1519 and had, in fact, established the Reformed Church. By 1529 Zwinglianism was the state religion in nine of the fourteen cantons. But then, deserted by the German Lutherans for theological reasons, Zwingli met military defeat in his struggles with the Catholics and fell in battle in 1531.

The France which Calvin had left in 1534, though it had no organized Protestant movement, did welcome ideas calling for the reformation of the Roman Church. Even in court circles religious reform was popular because there was as yet no reason for those who held such views to break with the Church. In 1516, even before Luther had posted his Ninety-five Theses, Guillaume Briconnet, the bishop of Meaux, had sponsored evangelical preaching in his diocese. Among his preachers was Farel, Calvin's predecessor and co-worker in Geneva. The reforms proposed by the Meaux circle, like those of Zwingli and Erasmus, were a product of an intelligent and moderate Christian humanism.

The French situation was unique because the effective administrative control of the Church was in the hands of the king. Persecution was intermittent and related to the needs of foreign policy rather than to religious conviction. The Affair of the Placards of 1534, when the rabble-rousing Protestants had attempted to split the French Church and, hence, France, did lead to more persistent persecution of Lutherans, but as late as 1536, when he dedicated the first edition of his *Institutes* to King Francis I of France, Calvin believed that the king could be won to his position and that reform within the Roman Church under royal leadership was possible. By this time, however, most Protestant activity had been driven underground or was moderated.

Switzerland and Geneva

The situation in Geneva in 1536 when Calvin arrived there was in many ways even less promising for sound religious reform than it was in Germany, German Switzerland, or even France. Geneva, not a part of the Swiss Confederation until the days of Napoleon, was a small "free city" of 17,000 which was under the alternating rule of a bishop and the Duke of Savoy. In 1525 and again in 1530 the Genevese had failed to gain their independence and escaped outright annexation by Savoy only because of the intervention of the Swiss city of Berne. Religion was not initially an issue in the struggle. However, in 1533, as the price of continued Bernese protection, the Syndics (City Commissioners) of Geneva were forced to accept Bernese Protestant missionaries, including Farel, Olivétan, and Saunier. As a result of this, religious riots broke out in Geneva and, for political reasons, Francis I prepared to help Savoy crush them when the Bernese in January, 1536, quickly defeated the duke and were able to take over Geneva and Lausanne. In May, 1536, the popular assembly of the town met in the Cathedral of St. Pierre and voted to become Protestant because this was the only way to avoid the return of the Duke of Savoy and the Bishop of Geneva. Obviously the vote was not based on deep religious convictions but it was in keeping with the character of the city. Genevese immorality was almost legendary.

The biography of Calvin in Geneva, which has been recounted separately, is also in large part the story of the development of Calvinism in Geneva and Switzerland. Many influences there were to color this development: the struggling republicanism of the people of Geneva; the heavy-handed missionary and political activities of Farel and Viret; the good judgment of Bullinger, Zwingli's son-in-law and successor in Zurich; and the creative theologians of Strassburg, particularly Calvin's teacher, Martin Bucer. Obviously the practices that were to exist in Geneva represented Calvin's ideas only in part. Only with the definitive edition of his *Institutes* and the progressive publication of his *Commentaries* and sermons was Calvinism finally defined. Calvin created a world and life view which won its own disciples. Calvin the man, however, had few.

The Protestant cantons of Switzerland which had been Zwinglian were the first area to accept Calvinism. In 1549 Bullinger and Calvin agreed in the Zurich Consensus to a common interpretation of the Lord's Supper, harmonizing the Zwinglian and Calvinist views. The other Protestant cantons except for Berne accepted this compromise. Not until 1580 did Berne abandon Lutheran consubstantiation. In 1566, two years after Calvin's death, the next step was made when a common Calvinistic confession of faith, the Second Helvetic, was accepted by Swiss Protestantism. This creed, a product of Bullinger's moderation, was later to be used in France, Hungary, Poland, Austria, Bohemia, and the Palatinate. Although bound by a common faith and a common creed, the Swiss Calvinistic churches never established a common ecclesiastical government. There was no general Swiss synod; each canton maintained its independent Reformed church. The maintaining of this independency within the framework of a common confession, which is a characteristic of Calvinistic churches, was perhaps even more unusual considering the seventy-five year conflict against the League of Catholic Cantons which followed.

For a time, because of their division and the corrupting influence of a Church-State relationship, the Swiss and Genevan churches lost their leadership of Calvinism to the Netherlands and Scotland. Great leaders such as Benedict and Francis Turretin, in preserving Calvinism from heresy, tended to reduce it to a tighter, scholastic system. Benedict was one of the leaders who insisted that the French-speaking Reformed churches must adopt the Canons of Dort, and Francis, his son and perhaps the greatest Swiss theologian after Calvin, sponsored the Helvetic Consensus which condemned the heretical views being taught in the Protestant faculty at Saumur in France.

In 1685, more than a century after Calvin's death, the Swiss churches were jolted to responsibility by the influx of perhaps a hundred thousand Calvinist refugees from France. The Huguenot refugees streamed over the frontiers following the revocation of the Edict of Nantes, a decree which had granted them a limited right to worship. These Huguenot refugees were to change the character of Swiss and Genevese Calvinism and society. Many French families were to become prominent in society, government, and commerce. They brought a refreshing urbanity to the somewhat isolated Swiss towns. They also brought with them the rationalism which was then popular in France, and a corrupted form of Calvinism. Soon these were to be characteristic of the Swiss Reformed churches as well. Jean Alphonse Turretin, the son of Francis, was to lead a movement to modify the strict orthodoxy of Swiss and Genevan Calvinism. This was accomplished by the abolition of the Helvetic Consensus in 1725. Thus not only were the Canons of Dort abandoned but also the theological foundation of the church itself, the Second Helvetic Confession.

The academy at Geneva founded by Calvin suddenly assumed new importance following the revocation of the Edict of Nantes because it was the only Protestant theological seminary in French-speaking Europe. It was soon, however, ignoring the creed and meddling with the catechism. By the eve of the French Revolution, a century later, Unitarianism in all but name had replaced Calvinism. The Trinity was openly denied and Predestination was condemned as being unacceptable in a rational world. Rousseau, who had been born of Reformed parents within sight of Calvin's cathedral, but was scarcely an orthodox Calvinist for all of that, took great delight in criticizing the heresy of the Genevan Reformed Church, which he considered to be little more than Deistic.

The French Revolution and the Napoleonic occupation of Switzerland did nothing to revive the Reformed churches. The rationalism of the Enlightenment remained dominant. Except for the influence of a few Moravian missionaries from Germany, vital Christian faith was almost unknown and orthodox Calvinism was a historical curiosity. Only with the peace following the Bourbon restoration did a change begin to take place. Ironically, orthodox Calvinism had to be replanted in Geneva, the birthplace of Calvinism, from abroad and the works of Calvin had to be rescued from oblivion by foreign money.

Beginning in 1815, for the first time in more than a quarter of a century, travelers were able to visit the continent freely. They were unprepared for what they found. During the time of restricted travel Britain and the United States had experienced the flowering of the Evangelical Movement, with its emphasis on orthodox theology, home and foreign missions, Bible and tract societies, and such social reforms as the anti-slavery movement and public education. To their dismay they found that the Continental churches had drifted in the opposite direction, rejecting even the vestige of their Reformation heritage. Everywhere the ministers seemed content to be government bureaucrats. Travelers wrote of searching France and Switzerland unsuccessfully for a single orthodox pastor and of being unable to purchase even one French Bible in the book stores.

One such visitor was the Scottish laird, Robert Haldane, Calvinist in theology but congregationalist in church polity, who arrived in Geneva in 1816 with his wife. He had earlier failed to find any orthodox Calvinist leaders in Northern France and was searching in French-speaking Switzerland. On the eve of what was to have been his departure from Geneva he met a student from the seminary who was fascinated by the things Haldane told him of British Christian developments. Soon this student and finally almost all the students of the seminary were meeting three times a week in Haldane's rooms to study Paul's letter to the church at Rome and to participate in what some of the students were later to call a seminar in Calvinism. This was strong meat for ministerial students who were never given even a course in the Bible itself and who had never read Calvin's writings. Obviously, neither the seminary faculty nor the city fathers, who maintained the established religion, approved such a venture and by indirect means brought the evening sessions to an end. However, the seeds of the *Réveil* (revival) had been planted and Calvin's writings and the Calvinistic creeds rescued from forgotten corners. Shortly after Haldane's departure from Geneva he was responsible not only for the republication of a French version of the Bible but also for a new edition of Calvin's *Institutes.*

During the same period his own commentaries on the Epistle to the Romans, which repeated the essence of his Genevan soirees, was also published. Later travelers were to leave their mark on Geneva but it was the seminary students and young pastors who had known Haldane who were to provide the basic leadership of the new Calvinism, not only in Switzerland but in France as well.

This Calvinism of the *Réveil* was more than the resuscitation of the Calvinism of the past. Its fundamental assumptions were the same and it attempted to reestablish the neglected creeds, but its conclusions were adapted to the vastly changed world of the nineteenth century. It was the beginning of a movement which, some fifteen years later, was to appear in the Netherlands' Reformed Church as the Secession of 1832. Salvation was made a matter of individual faith and not of citizenship nor even of baptism, the latter being by this time an accepted right of all citizens. This was a revolutionary conclusion in a Europe dominated by state churches. Increasingly, adherents of the *Réveil* demanded that the Church be separated from the State because, they contended, neither the government nor the society was Christian. This free church concept, more American than British, broke with the assumption accepted by the Reformers and Catholics alike, that Europe constituted a Christian society usually described as Christendom. The natural corollary of this break was a recognition that only a minority of the people of Europe were Christians in any sort of creedal or experimental sense. The new Calvinism therefore, made the believer recognize that his was the responsibility to evangelize not only Europe but the world. The *Réveil,* as a result, developed a series of evangelistic efforts ranging from Christian schools to foreign missions which, generally, matched the British and American efforts.

In Geneva the *Réveil* smoldered until the revolutions of 1830 made possible greater freedom of action. Meanwhile, the students and pastors who refused to submit to an 1817 gag rule against preaching about the Trinity, Original Sin, Grace, Effective Calling, and Predestination, either left Geneva or the church. One group which separated from the state church of Geneva was variously known as the Little Church and the Church of Bourg de Four. It was so highly experimental in its efforts to find a suitable Christian expression for its time that it was scarcely Calvinistic. Predominately lower class, it maintained a difficult but creative existence largely with foreign support. Its most distinctive characteristics came to be extreme independency and pietism. Some members even adopted the "plain clothes" usually associated with Mennonites. In spite of certain instability the Little Church was the first to launch missionary activity in France. create a theological school for the training of evangelists and missionaries, and establish a colporteur system.

A second center of *Réveil* worship was established in the home of César Malan, a young minister who was engaged primarily in teaching in a church-sponsored school. He had no desire to break with the state church but was mainly concerned with the reestablishment of Calvinistic purity. He defied the 1817 ban by quoting from the ancient Calvinistic creeds and catechism which had never been officially withdrawn. Only when no invitations were extended to him to preach in the churches of Geneva did he inaugurate meetings in his home and even then he avoided times which conflicted with the official church services. He effected no organization and did not administer the sacraments. Because of his caution and his genuine desire not to resist constituted authority, the Venerable Company of Pastors was slow to act against him and it succeeded in bringing about his resignation as a minister of the state church only in 1823. Even then Malan so opposed independency that he refused to join either the earlier *Réveil* group or the more respectable and Calvinist one which was to follow in 1830. Malan's ultra-Calvinist group was to remain an unaffiliated but anti-independent church until his death when, according to his will, the congregation was dissolved and the church edifice torn down. Malan's very considerable claim to fame was not as the author of a Malan-led Calvinistic revival, which did not materialize, but as a hymnologist. Virtually singlehandedly he transformed the musical concepts of the French Reformed churches. Churches which had closed their pulpits to his ministry even now sing his beautiful, reverent, Calvinist hymns, and the type of music he introduced still dominates French Reformed hymnology.

The epidemic of revolutions in 1830 unloosed the bond which had restrained man's liberty. The established church of Geneva which had maintained its position only with difficulty and with government repression, lost popular support. The men who had left Geneva rather than accept the ban of 1817 were able to return. Most prominent of these was Merle d'Aubigné, descendant of one of the greatest Huguenot families and, subsequently, the author of the most popular history of the Reformation. Having served as pastor of the Huguenot community in Berlin he was serving as pastor in Brussels under the patronage of the Dutch royal family when the revolution forced him to flee. Among those who followed him to Geneva were Antoine Galland, a man who had been heading the foreign missionary training school in Paris, and Louis Gaussen, probably the greatest French Protestant theologian of his time and the author of a major work on the plenary inspiration of the Scriptures. As ministers of the established church and as members of influential Genevan families, these men had a liberty that was denied the earlier *Réveil* leaders. Together with some prominent laymen these three formed the Evangelical Society of Geneva which soon was training ministers and evangelists, carrying on missionary work in France, distributing Bibles and evangelical books, and maintaining a place of worship which later developed into a free church. Liberal financial and moral support came from abroad and the Evangelical Society prospered. Although the Venerable Company of Pastors of Geneva was able to exclude these men from official pulpits in the canton, their influence increased and their evangelical Calvinism was increasingly accepted by ministers of the state church.

When the government entered the struggle between the Evangelical Society and the state church, the voice of Professor Alexandre Vinet of the neighboring canton of Vaud was raised in behalf of the free church. Vinet was the last of the great leaders of the Swiss *Réveil* to appear on the scene. He was a vigorous intellectual and a man broadly respected as a literary critic. His active defense of the *Réveil* brought him invitations not only to the chair of theology in the new theological school in Geneva but also to the editorship of a journal launched by the growing evangelical group in Paris.

Vinet hesitated. As a literary man perhaps he had not yet clearly defined his religious views. Even in historical perspective his theology is difficult to classify, but it certainly was not a completely orthodox Calvinism nor was it in full agreement with the *Réveil*. From time to time Vinet even protested against a church based on a creed, wishing to allow as much religious freedom to the individual as possible. He vigorously denied that religion was a matter of state legislation or of intellectual assent to an unintelligible creed; he asserted that it was, of necessity, a matter of individual conviction. Although he did not go as far as the German Schleiermacher and assert that religion is primarily a matter of feeling, Vinet left considerable room for religious sensibility. It was on the basis of these ideas that Vinet defended the absolute separation of Church and State. Vinet was, in fact, an anomaly in French-speaking Protestantism because he was aware of the dynamic theological changes taking place in Germany. He was to be virtually alone in this until the middle of the century.

After 1848 the autonomous development of the Swiss Reformed churches tended to end and their history to blend with that of European Protestantism. To be sure, the church in each canton had its own history but the developments were generally parallel. The *Réveil* lost its momentum as its ideas infiltrated the state churches, as the free church movement spread, and as its intellectual position became a defense against German heterodoxy. The conflict between those who considered adherence to a creed a matter of greatest importance and those who considered state control of religion the major issue, marked the second half of the nineteenth century. The leaders were not at first conscious of the extent to which German ideas were influencing the younger pastors and students. For the latter the conflicts of the previous generation were sterile. They found their stimulation in writings from Germany. Kant, Fichte, and Hegel gave them a new philosophical base. Even the least intellectual of them read the historical criticism of Strauss and his French imitator, Renan. Schleiermacher's works finally circulated in French. Ritschl's "social gospel" was received uncritically. The impact of scientific thought, of industrialization, and of general secularization made itself felt in the Reformed churches. Theological

Liberalism was on the throne. Gradually the free churches lost their vitality and the official churches were cast adrift by the governments of the cantons. History, not principle, kept them apart. Calvinistic orthodoxy lost ground gradually. It was to gain strength, but certainly not dominance, in the reaction against theological Liberalism immediately following World War I, the reaction marked by the growing neo-orthodoxy of Karl Barth and Emil Brunner, both of whom are in part products of Swiss Reformed life.

The German States

Although Calvin's personal influence was felt primarily in Geneva, in Switzerland, and in France, Calvinism was to have considerable influence in the area now known as Germany. There, among the more than two hundred states and cities which constituted the Holy Roman Empire, it was generally a continuation of Zwinglianism and was more generally in conflict with Lutheranism than with Catholicism.

Strassburg, a German free city on the Rhine, was the first to feel the impact of Calvinism. Its most influential leader between 1522 and 1552, Jacob Sturm, welcomed most Protestant ideas and most Protestant refugees. Among the latter was the great theologian Martin Bucer, who in 1530 after a decade under Lutheran influence was to write, with Wolfgang Capito, the first German Reformed confession of faith, the Tetrapolitanian or First Helvetic Confession. Twice Calvin was a refugee here, first in 1534, just after he fled from France, and again in 1538, when as a refugee from Geneva he served as peacemaker between the various Swiss Protestant groups which were struggling with the meaning of the sacraments. There also he met Melanchthon, the theological spokesman for Lutheranism, in an effort to unite all Protestantism. As the seat of such vigorous activity Strassburg was to waver between the Reformed and Lutheran camps for some time. In 1548, however, it accepted the Augsburg Interim, and this strengthened its Lutheran leanings. The final decision was deferred until 1577, when it accepted the Formula of Concord; but not until 1581 did it expel all Calvinists and Zwinglians.

Hesse, a major German principality which was to supply

red-coated mercenary soldiers to the British during the American Revolution, temporarily adopted Presbyterian church government without the other features of the Reformed tradition. In 1524 Landgrave Philip accepted Protestantism under the influence of Melanchthon and, shortly afterward, at the suggestion of Franz Lambert, a former Franciscan friar, established virtually the same form of church government which Calvin was later to advocate. At Luther's suggestion this form was abandoned for administration under the direct control of the margrave, but Reformed ideas were welcomed. It was at Marburg University in Hesse, in 1529, that Luther, Zwingli, and Bucer met in an unsuccessful attempt to develop a common Protestant creed. The following year, under the influence of Zwingli and Bucer, Philip refused to accept the Augsburg Confession. Not until the imperial Religious Peace of Augsburg in 1555 virtually outlawed Calvinism, was the Reformed influence excluded.

There was general interest in Reformed ideas in northwestern Germany, adjacent to the Netherlands. For instance, in Emden, bordering East Friesland, there developed the only Reformed church in Germany which was not originally Lutheran. The activities of Aportanus of the Brethren of the Common Life in 1526 and of Carlstadt in 1529 paved the way, but it was the Pole John Lasco, who had known both Zwingli and Calvin, who then established the Reformed church under the patronage of Count Christopher of Oldenberg.

The most important German Reformed movement was in the Palatinate, a major principality in southwestern Germany. Here from about 1545 to 1620 Calvinism flourished. Because the elector was friendly with the German emperor, the area did not become Protestant until late in the Reformation, in 1545. Legally the Peace of Augsburg of 1555, which closed the French Reformed Church that Calvin had served in Strassburg and ended Calvinist influence in Hesse, denied individual religious freedom in Germany and permitted the princes the right to choose only between Catholicism and Lutheranism for their territories. However, Elector Frederick III of the Palatinate, one of the seven electors of the Holy Roman Empire, was so disgusted by the controversy within Lutheranism that he welcomed Calvinistic ideas. High Lutheranism at the time was moving back toward Catholic practices, reintroducing Latin in the services and the veneration of the Virgin. Moderate Lutheranism led by Melanchthon was in retreat. In the face of this conflict, Elector Frederick invited Zwinglian and Calvinist teachers to come to the Palatinate. Under the influence of these men Elector Frederick moved the church of the Palatinate toward Calvinistic doctrine and practices without abandoning the Augsburg Confession. There were no feasts to the Virgin; altars, baptismal fonts, religious pictures, and even organs were removed; Latin was abandoned in all liturgy; and public and private morality was enforced.

Soon afterwards, the Elector commissioned Zacharias Ursinus, then twenty-eight, and Caspar Olevianus, only twenty-six, both teachers in his new University of Heidelberg, to draw up a confession of faith which, though basically Calvinistic, would avoid offending the moderate Lutherans. The German original of this confession, which has become known as the Heidelberg Catechism, was published in 1563. It skirted such controversial issues as the Lord's Supper and, in the first edition, even omitted Question 80, which condemns the Mass; it stated the doctrine of predestination in its mildest form, without reference to reprobation; and it seemed to teach universal rather than limited atonement.

In 1566 Frederick himself was forced to defend the Catechism before the Diet of the Holy Roman Empire (the German parliament) when he was charged with violating the Peace of Augsburg by having departed from Lutheranism. Not only did he give a brilliant defense but outside the sessions he gained an ally in Elector Augustus of Saxony, an adherent to Melanchthonian Lutheranism, who likewise feared possible repression by the advancing High Lutheran scholastics. Frederick defended the Catechism point by point, drawing only one protest and that from a Catholic bishop who disliked his comments on Question 80. The Diet recognized that Frederick's position was unique but, because he still held to the Augsburg Confession, it decided that he was not subject to deposition.

Unfortunately, even under Reformed influence, the Palatinate did not avoid theological controversies. The most famous of these was centered on Dr. Thomas Erastus, the court physician who disagreed on church polity with Olevianus, the most influential religious leader in the Palatinate. Erastus held that excommunication was the responsibility of the State and not of the Church. In the hands of his followers, Erastianism was expanded to require state supremancy in all ecclesiastical affairs. Erastus was forced into exile but his ideas were to recur wherever Calvinism was long dominated by the state.

Another controversy was the ancient one concerning the nature of the Trinity. Unitarians, or as they were known, Arians, and other religious dissenters looked on the Palatinate as a refuge. Three such Arian ministers, Neuser, Sylvanus, and Vehe, came under public censure. But one remained to be tried and he, in much the same manner as Servetus, was condemned to death by the synod and executed by Frederick. Another fled to the East, found there a view similar to his on the Godhead, became a Moslem, and subsequently was made a pasha.

The most serious controversy was over the Lutheran Formula of Concord of 1577, which represented extreme High Lutheran scholasticism and specifically excluded from fellowship those who accepted Calvinistic or Melanchthonian theology. The German princes who opposed this Formula attempted unsuccessfully at Frankfort am Main to create a Reformed formula of concord. The attempt to force all German Protestants to maintain the extreme position of the Formula created an unhappy situation wherever Calvinistic ideas had spread. Not until fifty years later was the problem resolved and then only in blood by the Thirty Years War.

Meanwhile, however, the Formula of Concord was so repugnant to many Lutherans, particularly the followers of Melanchthon, that dissenters found protection and freedom by becoming Reformed. For example, the Protestants of Nassau became Reformed in 1578, those of Bremen in 1581, of Zweibrucken in 1588, and of Anhalt in 1597. Not directly related to this reaction against the Formula was a significant change in Brandenburg-Prussia. There the Hohenzollern ruling family, which eventually was to unite Germany, adhered to the Reformed church in 1618 but, somewhat illogically, did not change the Lutheran religion of the state.

Almost overshadowed by these issues was a fourth which struck at the heart of the Reformation. In both Lutheran and Reformed circles there were efforts to modify the seeming arbitrariness in the doctrine of divine election. The Lutheran solution was simple — the virtual abandonment of the doctrine. The Reformed solution, however, was to soften and limit rather than abandon the doctrine. The first evidence of what was to be called Covenant, Federal, or Cocceian Theology can be found in the writings of Olevianus and, less well formed, of Ursinus. Its greatest champions, however, were Cocceius (John Kock) some fifty years later, Herman Witsius, and the English Puritans. Divine election, instead of being considered arbitrary, was based on an agreement (covenant) between God and Christ, or between God and the elect, by which God voluntarily limits His freedom and states His conditions of salvation. These conditions usually included faith, which for Calvinists remained a gift of God, and righteousness, which implied a moralism more legalistic than even Geneva had known. In Germany the Palatinate was the center of the development of Covenant Theology and, hence, the center of contention over the issue, and Palatinate Calvinists were to incur the anger of the Calvinists of Geneva and France for having departed from the teachings of Calvin.

Calvinism in the Palatinate as in all Germany maintained a constant struggle for its existence until the Peace of Westphalia in 1648 because it was, in fact, illegal. It was attacked by the Lutherans as vigorously as by the Catholics. In the Palatinate, Lutheranism was temporarily restored between 1576 and 1583.

The sad state of affairs was obvious during the opening phases of the Thirty Years War in 1618 and 1619. The revolting Protestants of Bohemia had chosen Elector Frederick V of the Palatinate as their king, a man who was the head of the Protestant Union as well as the son-in-law of James I, the Protestant king of England. Unfortunately, his ineptness, his Calvinism, and his wife's extreme clothes alienated not only the humble Lutherans of Bohemia but many of the Lutheran princes as well. The result was disastrous. Frederick was dubbed the "winter king" because he and his army melted away with the winter's snow. Calvinism, obviously, was not popular.

The war dragged on needlessly to satisfy the ambitions of France. Ironically, it was under the leadership of two Catholic cardinals, Richelieu and Mazarin, that France sided with the German Protestants. The Peace of Westphalia of 1648, which ended the war, was seemingly a victory for Calvinism because Calvinism was given equal status with Catholicism and Lutheranism in the Holy Roman Empire. However apparent the victory, the war had in fact undermined the Reformed churches. Because of the vagaries of the war, the Palatinate, the traditional German center of Calvinism, was divided, with the Upper Palatinate becoming Catholic. Not only Calvinism but all religion in Germany lost its vitality because it had been too long the basis of political and military struggle. Furthermore, because the Peace increased the authority of the princes at the expense of the emperor and the Empire, religion became increasingly provincial and subject to the whim of the multitude of princes.

The story of the German Reformed churches after 1648 is less than significant. In most areas all Protestant groups were forced into a common state-controlled Evangelical church. Theological as well as ecclesiastical differences were deliberately silenced in order to maintain political peace. The German Calvinistic church, where it continued to maintain its integrity, became a church of tradition rather than of creed. It lacked not only the unifying voice of a synod but, until 1871, even an informal German Calvinistic fellowship. It was open prey to heresy and heterodoxy. German Calvinism became a phase of the story of Lutheranism rather than of ecumenical Calvinism.

However minor the role of German Calvinism may be, the impact of German religious philosophy and of German Lutheran theology, as indicated earlier, on the Reformed Churches in Switzerland, France, the Netherlands, Britain, and America has been profound. These liberal ideas from Germany constituted the greatest challenge to the Calvinistic churches during the nineteenth and twentieth centuries.

France

The story of the Reformed church in France is inextricably linked to domestic and foreign politics. The church itself was to play such an important role that, for more than a hundred years, it was an armed state within a state interested more in political necessity than religious convictions. Under the circumstances it is understandable that the church became traditional rather than vital, self-consciously nationalistic and reluctant to participate in the main development of ecumenical Calvinism. To suggest that at one time more than half of the people of France may have supported the Reformed party implies what is not true, that the majority of the people were Calvinistic by religious conviction.

The future history of Protestantism in France had been presaged by the initial reception of Lutheran ideas about 1520. Even the sister of the king became an active supporter of proposals to reform the church, as did many nobles. Such support, it would seem, often arose out of political ambition rather than conviction. The subsequent intermittent persecution of the Protestants was likewise politically inspired, being based on royal attempts to win the support of the pope or of the German emperor. Generally the nobility were only slight ly touched by the persecution, however, with the brunt being borne by the middle and lower classes. This sharp class cleavage was to be perpetuated even in the French Reformed Church government, which gave the noble members separate and overriding authority.

With so many non-religious factors involved in the Protestant-Catholic struggle, it is understandable that the Protestants were slow to organize as a separate church. Only gradually were the remnants of the circle of Christian humanists at Meaux, the disciples of Luther, and the Calvinists drawn together. Under the inspiration of Geneva the first organized Reformed congregation was established in France, in Paris, in 1555. Four years later about fifty such churches joined in the first French national synod. This synod adopted a creed, a modification of a draft written in part by Calvin, and a book of discipline, which established not only the two class presbyterial or consistorial form of church government but also a pyramid of representative institutions above this level — colloquies or classes, provincial synods, and a national synod. This new church, staunchly Calvinist in theology, absorbed virtually all those groups which opposed Catholicism and became as important for its political as for its theological organization.

Curious episodes mark the period. In 1535 Francis I had invited Melanchthon to France in an effort to heal the religious breach. But the German princes, fearing for Melanchthon's safety, refused to permit him to go. The period after the ascension of Henry II in 1549, conversely, is usually considered a period of harsh persecution of Protestants as the result of the influence of the king's mistress, Diana of Poitiers, and of the Guise family. However, it was primarily the participation of Henry II on the Protestant side in the Schmalkaldic War which preserved German Protestantism and weakened the Catholic-Imperial cause. Another irony involved the marriage of Jeanne, Queen of Navarre and Protestant granddaughter of Francis I, to Anthony of Bourbon, head of the junior branch of the French royal family. This marriage in 1559 not only drew together the two royal branches but gave the Protestants two of their most redoubtable military leaders, Anthony, who became king of Navarre, and his brother, Louis, prince of Condé. The fact that neither man had particularly religious inclinations did not minimize the effectiveness of his military leadership.

Increased persecution caused the Reformed or, as they were subsequently known, the Huguenots, to take up arms in 1561 against the king. Calvin had opposed the war both before and after it had started but his voice was not heeded. The Huguenots, recruited primarily from the nobility and the new middle class of the towns, represented not only religious but regional and class interests. The war was bitter, sporadic and indecisive during the next forty years. Perhaps the most deplorable episodes were the St. Bartholomew's Day Massacre (1572) of thousands of Protestants on what was to have been a festival day to mark the union by marriage of the Protestant Bourbon and the Catholic Valois royal lines, the murder of Henry of Guise (1588), leader of the ultra-Catholic faction, and the murder of Henry III (1589). Such general extermination left only one man with a legitimate claim to the throne of France, Henry of Navarre, the leader of the Protestant faction. Recognizing after some time the reluctance of the people of northern France and particularly of Paris to accept him as a king as long as he remained Protestant, he changed his religion for the seventh time in his life and again became Catholic. The cynical comment "Paris is worth a Mass," though probably apocryphal, accurately represents his attitudes.

Nine years later, in 1598, after firmly establishing his own position, Henry, now Henry IV of France, issued the Edict of Nantes. This edict granted certain rights to Henry's former Huguenot comrades. It secured their political and military rights, but it granted considerably less than religious toleration. Reformed worship was permitted only in certain specified cities and on the estates of certain high nobles. Huguenots were, however, given equal right to public offices and, to guarantee these rights, the privilege of maintaining a state-paid private army as well as two hundred fortified cities. In many respects the Reformed church of France became a state within a state, bound to Catholic France only by a common loyalty to the king.

The era of the Edict of Nantes, 1589 to 1685, was marked by the burgeoning prosperity of the Huguenots and the gradual elimination of their rights. The attack on them was initially only against their political and military rights, which Cardinal Richelieu, the principal adviser to Louis XIII (1610-1643), insisted were a limitation on the sovereignty of the state and on the authority of the divinely appointed monarch. Three wars between 1621 and 1629 destroyed the Huguenots as an armed political party and left them merely a tolerated religious sect. Political peace, however, brought them great wealth. "Rich as a Huguenot" was a byword of the day. Theirs were the most characteristically capitalist and middle-class occupations of the day — commerce, banking, manufacturing, and shipping. Their ministers were famous for their eloquence but their schools were equally famous for their willingness to compromise with contemporary and Catholic thought. Many of the Reformed did, in fact, for convenience or conviction, become Roman Catholics.

Synods were abolished in 1659 by the king. However, as

late as 1675, Möise Amyraut, leader of the Protestant academy at Saumur and friend of the king, was able to use royal influence against his opponents who wished to force him and the other teachers of the academy to accept the Helvetic Consensus. Calvinistic orthodoxy, it would seem, was not a characteristic of the French Reformed Church on the eve of the revocation of Nantes.

Under the influence of his mistress, Madame de Maintenon, a Huguenot convert to Catholicism, and as a result of his own isolation in the splendor of Versailles, Louis XIV was convinced that persuasion and persecution had virtually eliminated Protestantism from France. He was utterly unprepared for what happened when he revoked the Edict of Nantes in 1685. France lost perhaps as many as a half million of her most able citizens and the leaders of her economic supremacy in Europe. More than twelve thousand soldiers and nine thousand sailors fled. In Touraine, a Huguenot center, 85 percent of the looms were made idle and 90 percent of the silk weavers fled. It is estimated that at least seventy-five thousand refugees migrated north, where they joined the French-speaking Walloon Reformed church in the Netherlands; one hundred thousand went to England and her colonies; seventy-five thousand to the German states; and twenty-five thousand to Switzerland. Most of the pastors fled and the nobles abjured their faith in large numbers to preserve their property. The Huguenots who remained were generally those without the money to flee, the peasant class. The new Reformed centers were the smallest agricultural villages. Many found refuge in the highlands of the Cévennes in southern France. Many more found safety in anonymity. Finally, in 1715, the last vestige of a legal status for non-Catholics was eliminated.

Between 1685 and 1789 the French Reformed Church struggled for survival. Isolated congregations and sometimes mass meetings met secretly, often on the mountain side or in open fields, to avoid the dragoons of the king. There was no ministry in the usual sense, and illiterate "prophets," who fell into trances, often took the role of preacher. Not until thirty years after the Revocation did the Church in the Desert recover sufficient vitality to reorganize, and even then the reorganization was primarily the work of one remarkable man, Antoine Court. Under his leadership, in 1715, when he was still less than twenty years old, the first of eight synods was held. Nine pastors were present at this meeting in a deserted quarry (three subsequently left the church for reasons of heresy or immoral conduct), and none had formal schooling or theological training. At least three were under twenty.

The subsequent and persistent persecution of the Protestants under Cardinal Fleury and immediately after his death made the second quarter of the eighteenth century as bitter as any the Protestants had yet faced. They lacked all civil rights, including the right to be born, to be married, or to be buried. Only the right to die seemed guaranteed by the state. To preserve some semblance of theological leadership Antoine Court in 1729 established a training school for pastors in Lausanne, Switzerland, to which courageous Frenchmen might flee for less than two years of education before returning to the oblivion of illegality. Fewer than half of the ninety who studied at the school during the century remained in the ministry. Semi-literate peasant pastors remained the norm of the Church in the Desert, and a member of the middle class like Paul Rabaut, who succeeded Court as the leader of the Reformed community, disdained the more humble pastors.

In France, unfortunately, the fires of persecution did not purify the church. The heroic struggle to reconstitute the organization of the church was not matched by a parallel struggle to restore Calvinistic orthodoxy. Until the middle of the seventeenth century violent prophetic utterances served as a substitute for a Scriptural ministry and, subsequently, in the better regulated congregations moralism took its place. Dogmatic loyalty to France, it would seem from the published sermons of the period, was more important than Reformed doctrine. Among the educated leaders the ideas of the Enlightenment came to be as generally accepted as they were in Geneva. Contemporary writers insist that the decline was so great that Huguenot was considered a legitimate synonym for Deist. In part because of this lack of sectarianism and in part because of the American example of religious liberty popularized by Lafayette, the king in 1787 issued an Edict of Toleration which permitted open Protestant worship and restored civil rights. This was, however, no sudden change. Anti-Protestant laws had been falling into desuetude since the middle of the century.

During the French Revolution, which began in 1789, the Reformed Church failed utterly to take a stand on religious principle. In fact, for some time the ideals of contemporary Protestantism were considered the same as the ideas of extreme Republicanism. The church, understandably, showed less vitality than it had a century before in the Desert. It lacked any theological moorings. Nor was there a resurgence after 1795 when the hiring of public halls for religious purposes again became possible. The large number of pastors, including Rabaut St. Etienne, previously the leader of the Reformed community, who had renounced the ministry and frequently Christianity itself, were reluctant to protest. Indeed, not even state support under Napoleon after 1802 resulted in more than a lethargic awakening. In 1801, after laborious negotiations, Napoleon had completed a concordat with the papacy which re-established Catholicism in France under the support of the government. In spite of the concordat Napoleon had no desire to become dependent on the Roman Church and, cleverly and dishonorably, modified the spirit of the concordat with the Organic Articles of 1802. The Articles were designed to implement the concordat, but in addition they re-established the Reformed and Lutheran churches and seminaries at government expense. Even Judaism was given a status of toleration. With Protestantism thus dependent on the generous whim of Napoleon, Protestants recognized that they must remain loyal to him to assure survival.

The Reformed Church, however, was almost unable to take advantage of the situation. Only 168 of the 220 clerical posts offered by the government could be filled and most of them only with men who were utterly unqualified. At this rate there was less than one pastor for each three thousand professed Reformed, approximately 2 percent of the population being Reformed. With freedom from military service one of the major attractions of the ministry, the sense of vocation of the seminary students was frequently less than convincing. It was subsequently necessary to draw on Huguenot and Swiss clergy from abroad to fill the pulpits. With local church government under the control of the wealthy landowners and with a denial of the right to call a national synod, the Reformed church was a weak but obedient creature of the state, led by ministers who yearned for episcopacy.

The revival of the French Reformed church after 1815 was a product of the same forces that led to the *Réveil* in Geneva and Switzerland. Obviously a religious revolution was necessary. This movement in France within a half century tripled the size of the Reformed community and gave it a vitality it had not known since the days of Calvin. Haldane's influence in France was not as dramatic as it had been in Geneva but it was important. After leaving Geneva, he lived for a time in Montauban in southern France where Napoleon had established one of the two Reformed seminaries. This one, which only a few years before had been forced to censor one of its professors for anti-trinitarianism, had become increasingly conscious of the dangers of Rationalism and Unitarianism. Haldane's influence gave support to nascent evangelical interest but primarily, to a revival of traditional Calvinism. His own vigorously Calvinistic commentaries on the Epistle to the Romans were given to each member of the graduating class of the seminary for more than thirty years. However, this situation was not entirely as it would seem because many of the more extreme Rationalists and Unitarians were also avowed republicans. This fact alone kept them in quiet disfavor and obscurity during the reigns of the restored Bourbon monarchs.

In Paris, where the Reformed community constituted a much smaller proportion than it did in the south of France but where many of the best educated and wealthiest were concentrated, the *Réveil* took root early. In 1818 under the leadership of an American merchant, S. V. S. Wilder, the first *Réveil* society, the Religious Tract Society, was founded. It was originally a motley group of Reformed and Lutherans, evangelical, indifferent, and Arian alike. In one respect alone were they similar — they represented the well-born and the wealthy. The following year substantially this same group of leaders established the Protestant Bible Society which soon was providing a free Bible to each child who completed confirmation classes. According to the royal charter of the Society, no Scriptures could be distributed to non-Protestants.

In 1822 these men founded still another society, the Foreign Mission Society, in the offices of Mr. Wilder. This Society was to send out as its first missionary an American, Dr. Jonas King, who was studying in Paris. It was in the training school established by this Society that the Genevan Antoine Galland, a disciple of Haldane, was to work out his internship before returning to Geneva in 1830 to spark the Evangelical Society there. In 1825 still another society was formed, the Society for the Encouragement of Primary Instruction among the Protestants in France. All these societies existed on the fringe of the official churches, though dominated by the leaders of those churches, and were characteristically Protestant rather than Reformed or Lutheran. In spite of the ambiguity of their official theological positions — the price paid to secure royal approval of their activities — they did furnish an outlet for *Réveil* activities.

The Revolution of 1830 was even more important in France than it was in Switzerland because the repressive measures were more severe. Almost immediately after the Revolution the evangelicals opened a center of worship on Rue Taitbout, not in an attempt to split from the official, state-supported Reformed Church but in a desire to maintain a ministry which they held was consistent with Scripture and the Reformed heritage. Many of the leaders of this chapel were also responsible for establishing in 1833 the French Evangelical Society which had as its purpose the conversion of French Catholics, and the French and Foreign Bible Society which, unlike the earlier Protestant Bible Society, did not limit its activities to the Reformed and Lutherans. These groups, because of their unquestioned theological stand, were generously supported by British and American churches, particularly those of the Calvinist heritage. Their activities were unquestionably effective in enlarging the Reformed churches but, understandably, led to Catholic counter-measures. Ministers, evangelists, and colporteurs working in Catholic areas were restricted and arrested. Religious guarantees in the hands of Catholic judges and administrators failed to result in religious freedom. Repeated papal encyclicals condemned not only the Protestant societies but the tracts and Bibles they circulated. Even Bible burning was again revived.

As in Geneva and Switzerland, contact between the French Reformed and their British and American counterparts resulted in a revitalized Calvinism. Most characteristically this took the form of creedalism, usually the demand that all the Reformed adhere again to the Creed of La Rochelle (1571). This revival of creedalism was originally intended to exclude the persistent strains of dying eighteenth century Rationalism — Unitarianism, Deism, and Socinianism. But it became increasingly popular when in the middle of the century not Rationalism but German-inspired theological Liberalism was recognized as the most serious challege to evangelical Calvinism. In 1872 the Calvinist Creed of La Rochelle was finally reaffirmed by the synod of the Reformed church. This, it would seem, marked the culmination af the *Réveil.* The victory, however, was more apparent than real because it resulted in a three-way schism of the church. The significant Free Church had splintered away in 1847.

Simultaneous with this trend toward confessional orthodoxy was a movement toward separation from the state. This was the French manifestation of the Free Church movement which had appeared elsewhere on the Continent. In France, however, the situation was even more complex than in Switzerland. Many of the greatest leaders of the *Réveil* opposed separation of the Church and State as did some of the most militant Liberals. Conversely, orthodox Calvinists cooperated with extreme Liberals in an effort to free the Church from government control and support. This cross-play of ecclesiastical and doctrinal issues was exceedingly disruptive in the French Reformed community and was resolved only in 1905, when a militantly secularist government terminated the link between Church and State for the Reformed as well as for the Lutherans and Catholics.

In spite of the victory of creedalism in 1872, German Liberalism became increasingly dominant in the French Reformed churches. Sons of the leaders of the *Réveil* appeared as leaders of what was subsequently known in America as Modernism. Calvinistic orthodoxy in France, as in Britain and America, was in retreat. Liberalism, however, was considerably more short-lived than in the Anglo-Saxon countries because few Frenchmen could continue to accept its optimism and its dreams of a better world after the gross devastation and atavism of World War I. The trend, however, was not back to the orthodoxy of the sixteenth century but to the Neo-orthodoxy of Karl Barth and Emil Brunner and to secularistic pragmatism. This disillusionment drove the French churches into union in 1938, the sister Reformed groups as well as the Evangelical and Reformed, the Congregationalists and Methodists. Perhaps more than in most countries the French Protestants have looked to such ecumenism as a basis for survival. Today only a few groups, including a small, orthodox Calvinist church, remain outside the united church, and Protestantism, along with religion in general, can claim little popularity in France.

Conclusion

During the four centuries after the Reformation, Calvinism in Switzerland, Germany, and France achieved glorious pinnacles of development and influence but in each area it subsequently floundered because of the inability of its adherents to cope with new problems as they arose.

The most persistent and demoralizing problem was that of the relation of the Church and State. The situation was seldom as neat as that described by Calvin in his *Institutes* because many governments though officially Christian were strongly anti-Calvinist and intolerant of any group which competed with the established state church. Calvin in his thinking did not countenance a permanently divided Church of Christ nor a Europe which was not basically Christian. For him, Lutherans and Catholics remained Christians however wrong their theology. Calvin left few hints for dealing with the situation as it was to develop. He affirmed Paul's statement that every Christian must submit to any government that maintained order, a conclusion rejected not only by the Calvinists of France and Germany but by those of Scotland and the Netherlands as well. He also maintained the necessity of a Free Church in a Christian society, but this ideal was not realized even in Geneva and found its logical culmination only in the nineteenth century Reformed and Presbyterian churches in America. In Geneva and the Swiss cantons the

Reformed church was made a department of the government, in Germany Calvinism had always been a creature of princely favor, while in France after existing as an armed political party for decades and then only as a disorganized underground movement, it became merely another bureau of the French government. Calvin's glorious vision of a Free Church in a Christian society had perished with the ascendancy of national monarchies and secularism. The church became either an instrument of or an enemy of the government.

The second major problem of the Calvinist churches in these countries was the lack of a clear, general voice. Calvinism became a tradition with a speechless present. Synods as working institutions were never established in Switzerland or Germany, while in France they maintained at best a troubled existence. In all these areas personalism and provincialism were frequent, even in matters of theology, and heresy was difficult to combat because there was no single voice of Calvinism. General acceptance of such basic statements as the Second Helvetic Confession, the Heidelberg Catechism, and the Canons of Dort was achieved by religious diplomacy rather than by the majority consent of the Calvinistic churches working through their Presbyterian principles. Only in the nationalist Reformed churches and in the Calvinistic sects did Presbyterian government find any consistent application and then, unfortunately, it worked against rather than for Calvin's hope of a united Calvinism if not of a united Christendom.

The third of the major problems of Calvinism in Switzerland, Germany, and France was a natural outgrowth of the first two. In all three areas salvation came to be assumed as the natural right of birth. In Calvinist Switzerland and in Germany baptism was presumed to assure salvation and was not only a right but an obligation of citizenship. In France, regardless of life, confession, or intellectual convictions, birth into a Huguenot family presumed not only membership in the Reformed Church but ultimately salvation. Heritage and not faith became the mark of a Christian. Understandably the reaffirmation of the doctrine of Salvation by Faith, which marked the Evangelical movement, the *Réveil,* and the Separation of 1832 in the Netherlands, re-established confessionalism and planted the seeds which were ultimately to destroy the concept of a state church and to revive the presbyterian form of Reformed church government.

BIBLIOGRAPHY

Bainton, Roland H., *The Reformation of the Sixteenth Century,* New York, 1952.

Baird, Henry M., *History of the Rise of the Huguenots,* 2 vols., New York, 1900.

——————, *The Huguenots and Henry of Navarre,* 2 vols., New York, 1909.

Cambridge Modern History: Vol. II, *The Reformation,* Cambridge, 1904; Vol. III, *The Wars of Religion,* Cambridge, 1905; Vol. IV, *The Thirty Years War,* Cambridge, 1906. These volumes consist of various essays by recognized authorities and are especially valuable on particular topics and events.

Good, James I., *Origin of the Reformed Church in Germany,* New York, 1881.

——————, *The History of the Reformed Church in Germany,* New York, 1894.

Grimm, Harold J., *The Reformation Era,* 1500-1650, New York, 1954.

Houghton, Louise S., *Handbook of French and Belgian Protestantism,* New York, 1919.
The brief historical section in this book provides not only a general survey of but also a guide through the hectic years of the nineteenth and twentieth centuries when French Protestantism was being torn apart by dissension.

Lucas, Henry S., *The Renaissance and the Reformation,* New York, 1934.

McNeill, John T., *The History and Character of Calvinism,* New York, 1954. This book provides not only a general history of the origin of Calvinism but also a sketch of the subsequent period.

3

THE HISTORY OF CALVINISM IN THE NETHERLANDS

The mother Church of Rome in the sixteenth century gave birth to several daughter churches. It was not a natural birth, but quite unnatural; it was an awful, painful, bloody birth. This unnatural birth would not have occurred if the Church had remained the faithful bride of her Lord and the faithful mother of her children, rearing them in the divine Word and Sacraments of her Lord. And so it was a tragic birth, for despite the most intimate, spiritual, and physical ties, the family of God was rent by schism, and the community of Christians torn asunder. In the Netherlands this schism led to a religious war in which the Gospel of Peace was defended with the sword.

Precursors of the Reformation

Faithful sons and daughters of the Catholic Church in the Netherlands had sought her reform in the centuries which preceded the Reformation. Notable examples of reform movements within the church were the societies of Beguines and the Brethren of the Common Life. Lay people played an important part in these reform actions. The Beguines were associations of lay men or lay women, freely associating in a communal form of life, to practice a simple, devout, and practical Christianity. Similarly, the Modern Devotion, founded by Floris Radewijns and Geert Groote in 1381-1382, was a society to help the laity to devote their lives to Christ, to separate themselves from the world and its temptations, to live a contemplative life, but one which was also productive and useful. In the clerk houses scribes copied precious manuscripts, and by the reproduction and distribution of religious literature helped to make religion more vital among the people. The monasteries of Groenendaal (1294, J.v.Ruysbroek) and Windesheim (1387, Geert Groote) were model institutions and encouraged monastic reform. The leaders of the Modern Devotion established religious schools where students from the coarse and uncivilized world were taught morals and the fear of God, and thus prepared for the cloisters and churches. The schools and monasteries of the Brethren stressed the mystic life of contemplation and the contemplative life found one of its finest literary expressions in the classic book of meditations *The Imitation of Christ* by Thomas á Kempis. The Brethren were marked by their stress on the importance of preaching; they called men to repentance and faith. In their schools learning was also promoted, especially classical studies. Great humanists like Wessel Gansfort and Erasmus were the products of these schools. These Christian humanists were quick to see the vices of the church and vocal in their protest against ecclesiastical corruption. The most illustrious of these humanists was Erasmus of Rotterdam, whose criticism of the church and society is recorded in *The Praise of Folly*. Erasmus's Latin translation of the New Testament from the original Greek and his new edition of the Greek text were important contributions to the Reformation. A critical attitude toward the doctrinal positions of the church had been expressed even earlier by Wessel Gansfort and Johannes Ruysbroeck. Gansfort had stressed the necessity of faith in those who received the sacraments; he was "heretical" in rejecting the infallibility of popes and councils and in his questioning of indulgences.

Altogether there were many factors which contributed to a growing revitalization and reform of Christianity within the Catholic Church in the Netherlands, and which, therefore, prepared a way for the Reformation. In summary, we note that there was first of all criticism of the doctrine and practice of the Catholic Church; secondly, an increasing emphasis upon simple, practical, Biblical Christianity; and lastly, a revival of preaching of the Word of God which had been almost entirely lost in the sacramentalist Church of Rome.

Origins of the Reformation in the Netherlands

Although Calvinism became the most important expression of the Reformation in the Netherlands, it was by no means the first in order of time. Very early the writings of Luther became known in the Lowlands, where they were widely read. The teachings of Luther were taught by Augustinian monks, and already in 1523 two of them, Hendrik Voes and Johan van Essen, were burned at the stake in Brussels for their heretical zeal and thus became the first martyrs to the faith. Despite the vigorous repressive measures of the Roman Church, Protestantism continued to gain many adherents. Some opposition to the views of Luther did, however, develop among a group of Protestants known as the Sacramentarians. These Sacramentarians denied the bodily presence of Christ in the sacrament and were inclined to regard Holy Communion as a remembrance. Prominent among the Sacramentarians was Cornelis Hoen, whose views on the sacrament of communion were posthumously published by none other than the Swiss reformer Zwingli (1525). The Sacramentarian views were preached by the priest Jan de Bakker, but he too was apprehended and condemned for heresy, and was put to death by strangulation and burning in 1526.

As early as 1521 edicts against Lutheran teachings had appeared in the Netherlands. Church and state were supposed to cooperate in wiping out heresy: the church prosecuted the heretic, the state executed him. The possessions of executed heretics were confiscated for the benefit of church, state, and informer. Since the Catholic clergy were initially not zealous in persecuting their erring brethren, the Pope sent three inquisitors to the Netherlands to do his ferreting out for him. The Sacramentarians were severely persecuted thereafter. In order to escape the Inquisition and to continue the proclamation of the gospel, the new preachers resorted to "field preaching" outside the city walls. Despite the heroism of preachers and believers, the Sacramentarian movement was short-lived because of inquisitorial persecution. After the Sacramentarians the Anabaptists became the principal proponents of the Reformation in the Netherlands.

The Anabaptistic movement, the so-called "Protestantism

of the Poor," was very strong for a time. These simple Protestants, who sought to actualize the Kingdom of God upon earth, tried to return to primitive Christianity, teaching community of goods and the equality of believers. They were millennialists who looked for the imminent return of Christ. The Anabaptists had a moderate and a radical faction; the former was led by Menno Simons, the latter by Melchior Hoffman. Whereas Simons favored freedom of conscience and non-resistance, Hoffman was intolerant of all but the "true" believers and sought to establish the Kingdom of God by the power of the sword. The Anabaptistic movement enjoyed the enthusiastic and even fanatical support of many Dutchmen during several decades. There was close contact with the radical Anabaptists in Germany; two Dutchmen, Jan Matthysen and Jan Beukelszoon, were leaders of the revolt in Münster. There the Anabaptists banished all who refused to be rebaptized. Militantly anti-Catholic, the Anabaptists removed images, paintings, and altar furnishings from the churches. Some of this militancy later became characteristic also of many Dutch Protestants. After the fall of Münster, the bastion of the radical Anabaptists, the Anabaptists were persecuted vigorously everywhere, and the movement in the Netherlands collapsed. The name Anabaptism became anathema to Catholics and Calvinists alike. The statement "wherefore we detest the Anabaptists and other seditious people," which occurs in Article 37 of the Belgic Confession (the first creedal formulary of the Dutch Calvinists), was motivated by the desire to distinguish Calvinism from radical Anabaptism.

The development of Calvinism in the Netherlands follows the collapse of the Lutheran, Sacramentarian, and Anabaptistic movements. The ascendancy of Calvinism in the Lowlands is in many respects a mystery, for the movement began to flourish precisely at a time when the Roman Church was persecuting Protestant heresy most vigorously. Despite the fact that persecution necessitated the establishment of Calvinistic congregations abroad (in Germany and England), Calvinism continued to gain adherents. It is literally true that the blood of martyrs was the seed of the Calvinist churches.

Calvinism developed first in the southern Netherlands, both in the Flemish and Walloon (French-speaking) regions. The successes of Calvinism were doubtless due in no small measure to its leaders, many of whom bear French names: Jean Crispin, Pierre Bruly, Vallerand Poullain, Jean Taffin, Martin Micron, and Guido de Brès. There were also others whose names have a solid Dutch ring (Petrus Datheen, Marnix van St. Aldegonde, Utenhove, *et al.*), but they were less numerous initially. Although John Calvin never visited the Netherlands, his influence there was profound, in part through personal contact with Reformed ministers who had studied at Geneva, and in part through correspondence with them. The writings of Calvin gained wide distribution and were also known by the common people. These writings were secretly distributed, being smuggled into the cities in vats, jugs, etc. Special colporteurs, men who distributed pamphlets, risked their lives in relaying such heretical literature to the people.

Because of the rigorous suppression of all forms of Protestantism in the Netherlands, the earliest Calvinistic congregations were formed in exile, beginning in the years 1548-1550. Such exile churches were organized in London, Emden, Frankfort am Main, and in the Palatinate. The Reformed Church at London was led by a Polish nobleman, Johannes ā Lasco, who was a great organizer; he was assisted by Delenus, Micron, and Utenhove. Already at this time, the preacher Utenhove was preparing a rimed version of the Psalms and a liturgy for the Dutch churches. With the accession of Mary to the throne in 1553, the Reformed congregation in London was compelled to move to the continent. Emden then became a center for Dutch Calvinists. At Emden a translation of the Bible was completed by 1562. The *Institutes* of Calvin were translated by Dyrkinus in 1560. A congregation of Reformed exiles also existed at Frankfort for a time, but Lutheran intolerance led to the banishment of these Calvinists. Perhaps the most prospering exile church existed in the Palatinate under the protection of Frederick the Pious. Here Petrus Dathenus prepared a translation of the Heidelberg Catechism. Dathenus was responsible also for the Dutch psalter (based on the French versification of the

Psalms), and the Reformed liturgical forms which continue to be used to this day.

From the outset the Dutch Reformed congregations became known as *De Kerken onder het Kruis,* that is, the Churches beneath the Cross. The name is significant, because it expresses the fact that despite persecution, churches — *organized* congregations — were established. Neither the Lutheran nor Anabaptistic movements succeeded in establishing a strong ecclesiastical organization. The Calvinists were a closely knit, well organized group of believers. The organizing ability of the Dutch Calvinists is generally regarded as one of the important factors not only in the establishment of the Reformed churches, but also in the success of the Dutch revolt against Spanish tyranny.

Obviously, the organization of Reformed churches in regions overwhelmingly Roman Catholic and hostile was a dangerous business. It took spiritual fortitude to become an active member of a church when the threat of death was constant. The Reformed churches were therefore initially "underground churches" and they developed some underground techniques appropriate to their situation, which was a struggle for survival. The identity of each church was kept anonymous by the use of secret names based upon the Bible. The church at Antwerp was the "vine," that at Doornik the "sword," and at Ghent the church went by the name "sun." After their heroic period the Dutch churches set a tradition by adopting such prosaic names as the old church, the new church, etc.

"The Churches under the Cross" were ministered to by itinerant preachers, but congregational leadership was provided by elders and deacons. Divine services were held in secret, usually at the homes of the various members of the congregation. Members were notified orally by a clerk of the time and place of meeting. The services were very simple, and often preceded by a common meal. The sermon was preceded by prayer and psalm-singing and was very often followed by the sacrament of communion. A collection was taken by the deacons, whose special task was to minister to the poor. Admittance into the church was upon confession of faith in Christ and the abjuring of popery. At times Roman

Catholics who had not yet broken with their church, but who were trustworthy, were admitted to divine services, but obviously this was exceedingly hazardous. Church membership was initially confined mostly to artisans and humble folk, though somewhat later wealthy merchants and lesser nobility joined the ranks of the faithful. Reformed churches were organized *before* there was a confessional statement, but nevertheless the congregations were strong and unified in their common confession of the Christ, in their faith in the Scriptures and in the sacraments of Baptism and Communion, and in the practice of Christian fellowship. Out of these small nuclei a strong and virile church was to grow despite the powerful opposition of an absolute state and church. Between 1550 and 1560 flourishing churches had developed in the southern Netherlands, in Antwerp, Ghent, and Doornik.

Needless to say, the organizing of churches posed many problems and the need for inter-church cooperation was keenly felt by the "Churches under the Cross." The Dutch churches received much assistance from the Reformed congregations at Emden, Germany. The Emden Church even received the name "The Mother Church of the Churches of God." The Dutch Calvinists felt the need of unity in confession and organization, and actively sought ecumenical unity, including unity with the Lutheran churches in Germany. In 1568 a meeting was held at Wesel in Germany to settle important questions pertaining to the offices in the church, the calling of ministers, the manner of preaching, house visitation, sick-calling, sacraments, marriage, discipline, and care of the poor. Although the problem of liturgy was left to the individual congregations, a recommendation concerning preaching was made, namely, that the sermons should be neither too long nor too speculative.

In general, however, attempts to gain support from German churches for the Calvinistic churches in the Netherlands were not very fruitful. Nor was it possible to achieve confessional unity; though the Calvinists were willing to accept the Augsberg Confession, they insisted on retaining as a symbol the Belgic Confession of de Brès, which had become the first creedal statement of the Dutch Calvinistic churches.

The German churches were also unwilling to support their Dutch brethren in the revolt against Spanish tyranny.

A national synod of the Dutch churches was finally arranged and met at Emden, Germany, in 1570. The various churches were to send authorized deputees, "in order to approve and decide on all that is presented in the common gatherings, as if you were all present together," as the circular letter of Marnix van St. Aldegonde phrased it.[1] Emden was the logical place for a meeting of the churches. After the coming of Duke Alva into the Netherlands in 1567 there had been another exodus of refugees. There were no less than six thousand exiles in Emden in 1570. When the synod convened in 1571 there were 19 ministers, 5 elders, 3 candidates, and 2 ministers emeritus present. The synod of Emden definitely established the organization and practice of the Dutch Reformed churches. The Presbyterian synodical organization was adopted, and every form of hierarchy was rejected: all Christians were regarded as brethren in the Lord. Though the Synod distinguished the offices of minister, elder, and deacon, the minister was not regarded as superior to the other officers of the church, nor was he to rule them, and he was equally subject to discipline. The Synod also favored the establishment of classes and national synods; however, it declared that these higher bodies could act only when the individual congregation was unable to settle a given problem. Thus the Synod of Emden was concerned to maintain the democratic character of the church; at the same time it showed real concern for the unity of the church. The actions of this synod in matters of organization were binding for the Dutch churches until the year 1816. The Synod also adopted the Belgic Confession and the Heidelberg Catechism as the creedal statements of the Reformed churches. In so doing, it also ended previous attempts to achieve a reconciliation between Lutheranism and Calvinism.

Another important topic of discussion at Emden was that of tolerance, that is, what attitude the churches should take toward non-Calvinists. On this difficult question opinions were

1. W. F. Dankbaar, *Hoogtepunten uit het Nederlandsche Calvinisme in de Zestiende Eeuw,* p. 65. In every instance the translation from the Dutch is my own.

divided, some desiring to compel conversion at the point of the sword, and others advocating freedom of conscience for Roman Catholics and other Protestant groups. This thorny problem continued to plague the churches for decades, for in seeking to gain religious freedom, the Calvinists were compelled to co-operate with both Roman Catholics and Humanists.

The Synod of Emden was not exclusively occupied with theological and ecclesiastical questions. Following the practice of previous synods, it concerned itself with many practical problems as well. The synods forbade certain names for the newly born and regulated funerals, dealt with begging, adultery, and drunkenness, gave attention to civil marriage and divorce, had something to say on clothing, vocational training, employment problems, the printing press, commerce, and alchemy.

The need for such all-embracing legislation was the more necessary and urgent because of the peculiar relation of the church to the government. In Germany, where conditions were stabilized, the policy was: *cuius regio, eius religio,* that is, the religion of the ruler is the religion of the people. The Netherlands, however, were in a state of war; the provinces had revolted against Spain. In this revolt the Calvinists were playing a dominant role. (Humanists, Roman Catholics, and Calvinists were united in resisting Spanish suppression, though for different reasons.) Thus in 1572 the *Geuzen* (Dutch Sea Beggars), who were Protestant if not Calvinistic, took the initiative in raiding Spanish shipping and succeeded in seizing several important coastal cities. Once a city was captured it was up to the rebels not only to set terms of surrender but also to determine policy with regard to the populace. Capitulation to the *Geuzen* usually meant that the Roman religion would be tolerated, but in practice these agreements were often ignored. The *Geuzen* appointed Calvinistic magistrates, procured churches for the Calvinists, secularized cloisters (using funds for the support of the government and the Reformed church), and usually forbade the public practice of the Catholic religion. Catholic churches were modified to accommodate Protestant religious practice: images, altars, and pictures were removed. Often the treatment of Roman Catholics was harsh and even cruel. We should bear in mind, however, that the Calvinists constituted a small minority group; certainly their numbers did not total more than one-tenth of the population. Roman Catholics were often like a fifth column within the Protestant camp. Whereas in Germany 80 percent of the Roman clergy became Protestant in Protestant states, in the Netherlands not more than 5 to 10 percent of the priests embraced Protestantism (i.e., Calvinism). In the measure that the war against Spain was successful, mutual tolerance between Calvinists and Catholics became impossible. This was all the more so because Calvinists looked upon Catholicism as a false religion, an "accursed idolatry" (cf. Heidelberg Catechism, XXX).

Although a minority group, the Dutch Calvinists were leaders in the revolt, and where the revolution succeeded, there Calvinism became the official religion and received the sanction and support of the state. And it was due in no small measure to this favored position of the Calvinists that the consolidation and expansion of the Reformed churches could take place after 1570. Calvinism was able to expand because of its close ties with the government, but this relationship was also detrimental and posed serious problems for the churches. Before we comment on the unfortunate results of this necessary, but "unholy" alliance between Calvinists and non-Calvinists in the revolt against Spain, we must call attention to the first great Calvinist leader and briefly indicate how the Calvinists became involved in the war for freedom.

The "Reformer of the Netherlands" is Guido de Brès (also De Bray), born at Bergen in 1522. Between his eighteenth and twenty-fifth year De Brès was converted to the Reformed faith through the reading of the Bible and Reformation literature, and he became the leader of Dutch Calvinism in its formative stages. The spirit of this "Minister of the Word of God in the Netherlands" (Datheen's designation) is evident from a letter written to his mother shortly before his execution as a heretic in 1566. In this letter he says:

> You asked that the son you bore in your womb might be a Jesuit; God has indeed made of him a Jesuit, but not of that new sect, which people call the Jesuits. Having made me a true follower of Jesus, the Son of God, He has called me to His holy service, not to teach the doc-

> trine of men, but to preach the pure and simple words of Jesus and His apostles. May it not be difficult for you, that God now wishes to receive me as a sweet-savouring sacrifice and by my death to fortify the people whom He has chosen.[2]

In 1552 De Brès was an itinerant preacher in the southern Netherlands. Practical in his preaching, he emphasized compassion, not only toward those of the household of faith, but also toward those outside. In 1555 De Brès published an apology of the new faith entitled *Bastion of the Christian Faith,* in which he attacked the infallibility of popes and councils and rejected the Roman practices of celibacy and saint and relic veneration. De Brès taught that the marks of the true church were the pure preaching of the word, and the administration of the sacraments of communion and baptism. In 1561 he preached outside the walls of the cities Doornik, Rijssel, and Valenciennes. So powerful were his sermons that the people of Doornik were inspired to sing Psalms in the streets. This constituted an open act of rebellion in the eyes of the Catholic regentess Margaret, who sent commissioners to investigate. De Brès was forced to flee, but the commissioners seized his writings. Indeed, while they were still in the city, a package addressed to the King of Spain was thrown over the city wall. The package contained the Belgic Confession and an Apology to the King. The Apology stated that the Confession was prepared "by common consent of the believers who are dispersed in the Netherlands, who desire to live according to the purity of the Holy Gospel of our Lord Jesus Christ."[3] In his Apology De Brès protests that the Reformed Christians are not seeking to overthrow the government, but rather to maintain the Christian faith, which the sovereign was also duty-bound by oath to uphold. The Apology is a touching commentary upon the grievous circumstances of the Reformed Christians. De Brès calls upon his sovereign to terminate the bloody persecutions, saying:

> For how reprehensible, if thou stretch forth thy arm in order to soak and wash it in the blood of so many

2. *Ibid.,* p. 10.
3. *Ibid.,* p. 14.

> people; O God, what destruction you shall cause your subjects, what wounds to your people, what lamentations, what sighs, what groaning of women, of children, of maidens, and friends; what eye can remain dry and not bathe in tears at the sight of so many noble citizens, beloved by everyone, hated by no one, who, after being cast into dark and horrible prisons, after suffering and tribulation, are subjected to torments and a scandalous death, the most cruel and awful ever conceived by pagan and unholy tyrants. And the women, if they are able to escape death, are condemned to wander in foreign lands, with their little children at their necks, begging bread from door to door. O gracious Lord, may our posterity not describe your realm as bloody and cruel. May they not say that the honor of thy grand-parents, the nobility of thy father, and thy own virtues and piety were darkened by a cruelty, a cruelty which I say is natural to beasts, but beneath the dignity of human beings, and most unworthy in a prince and ruler in whom nobility and especially piety consist above all in loving kindness and meekness, which are a true mark and a genuine distinction between a real king and a tyrant.[4]

The Belgic Confession which accompanied this Apology is doubtless unique among Calvinistic creedal statements. Already in 1562 it was accepted as the official creed of the Netherlands Reformed churches. Its author, De Brès, whose eloquence may be judged from the Apology, continued his effective preaching until 1566; and under his influence the number of Calvinists in the southern Netherlands grew until they were actually dominant in such cities as Doornik and Valenciennes. In his field-preaching De Brès was assisted by Peregrin de la Grange and Jean Cateaux. Each day they preached outside the city gates, administered the sacraments, performed marriage ceremonies, and led funerals. As a result of such effective preaching, and in reaction to the brutal suppression of Calvinism, the crowds were becoming restive. Their situation was unbearable, but the government would make no concessions: no churches were permitted and the Reformed religion remained banned. Finally, a large group of nobles petitioned the regentess for moderation in the placards

4. *Ibid.*, p. 21.

against heresy. Despite her promise, the regentess did not moderate the anti-Protestant edicts. The people cynically spoke of the edict of moderation as the "edict of murderation."

But repression had now been carried too far, and suddenly there was an open revolt: the iconoclastic riots of 1566. In the cities, the churches were stormed, images and altars were destroyed, and all that was "idolatrous" in the Roman churches (some 400 of them) came under the sledge-hammers and axes of the infuriated mobs. Although without apparent leadership, the mobs were singularly successful and the riots quickly spread throughout the land. Hundreds of churches were ruined, priceless art treasures were destroyed. There is no indication, however, that any property was stolen.

Such a rebellious act called for drastic action on the part of the government. The city of Valenciennes, a center of the Calvinist faith, was besieged. Though De Brès and de la Grange succeeded in escaping over the city walls, they were soon apprehended. Several months later these heroic preachers suffered a martyr's death for their convictions.

The bloody suppression of the iconoclastic riots convinced the consistories of the Reformed churches in the southern Netherlands that freedom of religion could not be obtained through petition, and after 1566 they decided that their only salvation lay in resorting to force. However, the severe repressive measures of the Spanish general Duke Alva made any action on the part of the consistories impossible between 1567-1572. Again there was an exodus of Calvinists abroad, now mainly to Germany. The future leaders of the Dutch revolt, the Prince of Orange and Marnix van St. Aldegonde also succeeded in making their escape, thus avoiding the fate of the counts Egmont and Hoorne, who, though Roman Catholic and the highest officials in the land, were beheaded at Alva's orders.

The question of the right to revolt was an important one among Dutch Calvinists. They were convinced that religious and political questions were inseparable. And the Scriptures demanded obedience to the civil magistrate. May one rebel against God-ordained authority? The vexing problem had first come up in connection with the public execution of heretics. Such public executions, we should note, did not have the desired effect, for although the executions by strangling and burning were horrible, the tranquility and transcendent faith of many martyrs was often a source of inspiration to other believers and onlookers. It is significant that in these dark days the books of martyrs began to appear. These were inspirational books, and next to the Bible, no other books were so widely read. The martyr deaths, however, did not always produce a spirit of heroic acquiescence. On the contrary, sometimes the public became aroused, and even sought forcibly to free the victims of the inquisition. Was this justified? Calvinistic congregations sought advice abroad, but the answers were negative. Must the Christian then suffer every injustice? Must the practices of the "godless" Roman Church be tolerated?

In answer to these questions there gradually developed a theory of the right to revolt, a right based upon Biblical and historical considerations. Rebellion came to be regarded as lawful when it was pursued through legal channels; revolt was permissible when the *magistrate* defended the rights of the people over against a tyrant; it was justified when the true religion was being suppressed by a false religion. And thus an alliance developed between the Calvinistic consistories and the magistracy, that is, the nobility represented in the States General and the Stadtholder of the King.

This matter of a legal revolt may be clarified by considering the status of Prince William of Orange. He was a hereditary count of Antwerp, member of the Brabantic States, Stadtholder of Holland and Zeeland, knight of the Golden Fleece, and one of the King's highest representatives. He was obliged by oath, in the name of the king, to protect the people and to maintain the privileges which they had secured throughout the centuries. What was the prince to do when the king violated these privileges and destroyed the people? In this situation the prince felt obligated by his oath to defend the people against their tyrannical lord, and thus he actually became the leader of the Dutch revolt.

This theory of revolt was set forth in an essay by Philippe du Plessis Mornay and Hubert Languet, entitled *Vindiciae contra Tyrannos,* and published in 1579. According to this theory the sovereign rules by divine right but he makes a compact with the people whereby they accept him as sovereign and he agrees to defend the rights of the people. This theory comes to expression in the Edict of Secession of 1581, where we read:

> Since it is known to all that a Prince of the land, by the authority of God, is head of his subjects in order to guard and to protect them from all inequality, molestation and violence, like a shepherd safeguarding his sheep, and that the subjects were not created by God for the benefit of the Prince, in order to be subject to him and to serve him as slaves in all that he commands, whether right or wrong, but that the Prince was created for the sake of his subjects, without whom he is no prince, in order to rule them with justice and reason, and to lead and to love them as a father does his children, and a shepherd his sheep, who risks his life in order to save them, and when he does not do this, and rather than protecting his subjects, seeks to suppress them, to burden them, to withdraw their ancient freedoms, privileges and existence, and to order and use them as slaves, he is not to be regarded as a prince, but as a tyrant, and such a person may no longer be regarded as a prince, at least not by his subjects, especially after deliberation by the States General, but they may leave him, and without doing wrong they may choose in his stead another as a leader for their protection.[5]

Thus Calvinism in the Netherlands developed a political theory which justified the right to revolt. The Calvinistic concept of the state is also defined in the Belgic Confession in Article 36, which originally read:

> Their office is not only to have regard unto and watch for the welfare of the civil state, but also that they protect the sacred ministry, and thus they may remove and prevent all idolatry and false worship, that the Kingdom of Anti-Christ may be thus destroyed and the Kingdom of Christ promoted.[6]

According to the Dutch Calvinists, therefore, the Spanish monarch was culpable on at least two counts: he was a tyrant

5. *Ibid.*, pp. 107-108.
6. Cf. *Psalter Hymnal*, "Doctrinal Standards and Liturgy of the Christian Reformed Church," p. 19 of the Supplement.

in withdrawing privileges and suppressing the people; he was apostate in seeking to maintain a false religion. Thus the cause of Calvinism and that of the Republic were fused and united. This union, which resulted eventually in the ascendancy of Calvinism and the founding of the new Republic of the Netherlands, was fraught with dangers to the official Reformed Church.

Although the revolt against Spanish tyranny had begun as an alliance of Calvinists, Humanists, and Roman Catholics, this alliance could not endure. The problem of religious tolerance became an insuperable barrier to political unity, since the Roman Catholic Church retained the allegiance of a vast majority of the people. Attempts to arrive at a settlement by making either Calvinism or Romanism the official religion on a regional basis were only partially successful. Thus in 1579 Catholicism was officially accepted in the southern Netherlands (Union of Atrecht) and Calvinism in the northern Netherlands (Union of Utrecht), and dissenters in each area were to be tolerated. When, however, the Spanish forces succeeded in subduing the southern provinces and captured Antwerp in 1585, the northern and southern Netherlands were permanently separated, the South becoming Catholic and the North Protestant. Calvinism, which had enjoyed its initial triumphs in the southern provinces, now was restricted to the northern provinces. These northern provinces successfully continued the war against Spain, achieving final independence by the Treaty of Westphalia in 1648. After 1585 the northern provinces began to prosper and Calvinism began its grand expansion. To this day the religion of the southern Netherlands (Brabant and Limburg) and Belgium is almost exclusively Roman Catholic.

Another major contribution to Dutch culture in which Calvinism shared was the founding of Leyden University in 1575. In reward for the valiant defense of their city by the Leyden citizenry, Prince William of Orange ordered the establishment of a university in Leyden. The need for a university in the Netherlands was urgent; education could not stop, for despite the war important posts in government and church would have to be filled. The motivation for the establishment of the Leyden University was expressed as follows by the Prince:

> Therefore as a firm support and buttress of freedom and good lawful government of the land, not only in matters of religion, but also in that which pertains to the common civic welfare, it is necessary in particular and above all else that here within the country in the counties of Holland or Zeeland, a good, adequate and reputable school or university be established, where the youth of the aforementioned countries, as well as those of Brabant, Flanders and other nearby lands may be educated in the right knowledge of God and all kinds of good, honest, and liberal arts and sciences, being of service to the lawful government of these lands.[7]

Speaking of the Calvinists' interest in higher education Dankbaar says: "The Calvinists were glad to recognize a free science and philosophy as the product of the divine *gratia universalis;* and acknowledging the sovereignty of God, they promoted every science which might be of service to the church."[8] Although the growth of Leyden University was initially slow, the school achieved increasing prominence in the world of learning in the seventeenth century.

The training of Calvinistic preachers was to take place at Leyden University. However, the problem of church-state relations became awkward and difficult at once, for the control of the university was vested in the magistrate, who also made appointments to the department of theology. This, we should add, was done over the protests of the Calvinistic clergy, whose repeated remonstrances did not intimidate the magistracy, but only confirmed its obduracy in this matter. The magistrates, many of whom were only nominally Reformed, desired that the university should be free from ecclesiastical control. Indeed, the magistrates argued that since they belonged to the Reformed church, their right to make appointments should not be a cause for concern. The magistrates, even when they were Calvinists, were very jealous of their prerogatives, and were able to retain control of the university. In this way, too, the "unholy" alliance between church and state was confirmed, and one of the causes of the

7. Dankbaar, *op. cit.,* p. 133.
8. *Ibid.,* pp. 141-142.

ascendance of Calvinism was to become a contributing factor to its decline.

Although the several departments of the University presently began to flourish, the theological department was wanting in candidates. Upon appeal of the clergy the magistracy in 1592 agreed to set up a *Collegium Theologicum,* a government supported seminary for needy theological students. The close tie between state and church is evident in the reasons for the establishment of this institution. It was established, so we read

> to the honor of God, for the upbuilding of the Church of Christ, in order that with thorough knowledge and unity the Christian reformed religion may be more profitably taught and practiced within these lands for the edification and instruction of the congregation and the derogation of all error and heresy within these lands.[9]

These hopeful aims that the "Christian reformed religion" might be promoted and error eliminated proved vain. In 1602 the magistracy appointed to the theological faculty of Leyden University Professor Arminius, and it did so over the protests of the Calvinist clergy, who had reason to suspect the orthodoxy of this theologian. Arminius soon became embroiled in polemics with his more orthodox colleague Gomarus. The controversy dealt with the questions of predestination and free will, total depravity and human responsibility. Discussion was not limited to academic halls, but descended into the public streets. The death of Arminius in 1609 did not end the dispute, for the followers of Arminius, the Remonstrants, became increasingly vocal and active in promoting Arminian doctrines, and their opponents, the Contra-Remonstrants, were no less diligent in their defense of orthodox Calvinism. The Calvinistic clergy demanded that the magistracy, the highest authority in the land, call a national synod where the theological issues might be debated and settled. The question was now no longer a theological one, but had become a political problem concerned not only with freedom of conscience but also with the authority of the magistracy in ecclesiastical affairs. The theological controversy

9. *Ibid.,* p. 154.

inevitably degenerated into a political battle which even involved the issue of the sovereignty of the individual provinces in relation to the stadtholder. Prince Maurice sided with the orthodox divines and gained political and military control over the country. The elder statesman Johan van Oldenbarnevelt, who was the leader of the magistracy, and who had for forty years served the Dutch republic, now became the victim of harsh justice and was beheaded on the charge of treason. With his death, the party of the prince (and the orthodox Calvinists) became dominant, and the national synod could be called.

This Synod of Dort (1618-1619) debated and rejected the theological views of the Arminians and gave classic formulation to the Calvinistic doctrine of the sovereignty of God in election and reprobation:

That some receive the gift of faith from God, and others do not receive it, proceeds from God's eternal decree,

> according to which decree He graciously softens the hearts of the elect, however obstinate, and inclines them to believe; while He leaves the non-elect in His just judgment to their own wickedness and obduracy.[11]

The Canons of Dort certainly should be read in the light of their concluding statement in which the Arminian misrepresentation of the orthodox doctrine of predestination is pointedly stated. The Synod rejected the following Arminian construction of predestination:

> That the doctrine of the Reformed churches concerning predestination, and the points annexed to it, by its own genius and necessary tendency, leads off the minds of men from all piety and religion; that it is an opiate administered by the flesh and the devil, and the stronghold of Satan, where he lies in wait for all and from which he wounds multitudes and mortally strikes through many with the darts both of despair and security; that it makes God the author of sin, unjust, tyrannical, hypocritical; that it is nothing more than interpolated Stoicism, Manicheism, Libertinism, Turcism; that it renders men car-

11. Canons of Dort, I, 6. The translation used is that found in the *Psalter Hymnal.*

> nally secure, since they are persuaded by it that nothing can hinder the salvation of the elect, let them live as they please, and therefore that they may safely perpetrate every species of the most atrocious crimes; and that, if the reprobate should even perform truly all the works of the saints, their obedience would not in the least contribute to their salvation; that the same doctrine teaches that God, by a mere arbitrary act of his will, without the least respect or view to any sin, has predestinated the greatest part of the world to eternal damnation and has created them for this very purpose; that in the same manner in which the election is the fountain and the cause of faith and good works, reprobation is the cause of unbelief and impiety; that many children of the faithful are torn, guiltless, from their mothers' breasts and tyrannically plunged into hell; so, that neither baptism nor the prayers of the Church at their baptism can at all profit by them.[12]

The Synod went on to say that it rejected "many other things of the same kind, which the Reformed Churches not only do not acknowledge, but even detest with their whole soul."[13]

The Synod of Dort is a symbol of the triumph of orthodox Calvinism in the Netherlands. The orthodox Calvinistic position was now clearly defined and became the teaching of the official Reformed churches in the Netherlands. And since the Reformed churches were the official, if not the state church, it was the duty of the state to uphold the true religion. Consequently, all Arminian pastors were banned from the pulpit. Some two hundred of them were deposed. Many of them went into exile, others went "underground," and some recanted their errors. Thus orthodox Calvinism, thanks to its controlling power in the state, was able to maintain purity of doctrine in the official church of the land. In the Calvinistic state of the Netherlands dissenters (and Roman Catholics) were allowed limited freedom of religion; they were given freedom of conscience and speech, and afforded the right to practice their religion in a private, inconspicuous manner. Only Calvinism might be publicly propagated. Although Cal-

12. *Ibid.*, "Conclusion." The translation used is that found in *The Psalter*, revised edition, Wm. B. Eerdmans Publishing Co., 1947.

vinism did not bring complete freedom of religion, it achieved a measure of freedom of conscience which was unparalleled in seventeenth century Europe.

With the triumph of orthodox Calvinism the process of evangelizing the northern Netherlands could continue. The Calvinists pursued this objective devotedly and determinedly. Their efforts were richly rewarded, for by the middle of the seventeenth century one-half of the Dutch people belonged to the Reformed Church of the Netherlands.

Summarizing, we note that Calvinism in the Netherlands developed despite opposition and persecution. It became associated very early with the struggle for freedom. Calvinists demanded the right to worship God in obedience to His Word. They developed a theory of revolt and struggled for religious and political freedom. The hard core of resistance in the battle against Spanish tyranny was formed by the Calvinists, men stalwart in the faith, willing to face insuperable odds, because of their belief in God, divine revelation, and divine grace in their lives. Although Calvinism appeared late on the Netherlands scene, it enjoyed a unique triumph there. Factors which are important in explaining the phenomenal rise of Dutch Calvinism include:

(1) The heroic personality and dynamic conviction of its preachers and leaders.
(2) The organizing power and ability of the Calvinistic congregations.
(3) Calvinistic contributions and leadership in the war against Spain.
(4) Calvinistic interest in higher learning; trained ministry.
(5) Close ties between church and state in the seventeenth century.
(6) Power of God's Word in the lives of believers.

Indeed, we may say of the Dutch Calvinists in this period of their nascence and florescence, that they "took their stand with truth as their belt, righteousness as their breastplate, the gospel of peace firmly on their feet, salvation as their helmet, and in their hand the sword of faith, the Word of God."

Decadence and Renascence of Dutch Calvinism

The Synod of Dordrecht marked the ascendancy and establishment of the orthodox Reformed religion in the Netherlands. In formulating the Canons of Dort the Reformed churches gave definitive expression to the orthodox Reformed conception of the absolute priority of divine sovereignty and grace in the salvation of sinful man. In the Canons Reformed theologians defined orthodoxy; the sign of orthodoxy hereafter was adherence to the doctrines of (1) the total depravity of man, (2) unconditional election unto grace, (3) limited atonement, (4) irresistible grace, and (5) perseverance of the saints. The history of Dutch orthodox Calvinism after 1618 is largely an attempt by the established church to maintain doctrinal purity as defined in the creedal statements: The Canons of Dort, the Belgic Confession, and the Heidelberg Catechism. The Canons, adopted only after prolonged and painful polemic within the church, remained the most controversial creedal statement of the Reformed churches. Increasingly, the Canons became a dead letter in the church, until finally in 1816 by state decree the Canons were dropped as a creedal statement of the *Hervormde Kerken.*

After 1618 the Dutch Reformed Church enjoyed the sanction and support of the government in a state which was officially Protestant Christian. The Synod of Dordrecht convened not only with the approval of the state, but also with its financial support, the entire cost being absorbed by the state. The Synod undertook, with state approval and at state expense, the costly translation of the Bible from the original tongues into the Dutch language. Accordingly, this translation was designated the *Statenbijbel,* that is, the "States Bible." Thus the *Statenbijbel* (translation completed in 1637) itself reflects the close ties between church and state. The interest of the magistracy in the true Reformed religion is well expressed in the foreword to this famous Bible translation:

> Greetings to all who shall see this or hear it read: they are informed that from the outset we have taken the reformation of these lands to heart, and have tried with all diligence and care to order all things which might promote the well-being and the prosperity of the genuine, true Christian Reformed religion.

Thanks to its preferred status, the Dutch Reformed Church was able to pursue its policy of evangelizing the nation. Directly or indirectly the church controlled the educational system, this control being particularly effective at the lower, local levels. The state-financed schools were generally staffed by teachers of Reformed conviction so that these institutions were in effect Christian (Reformed) schools.

The real problem, as we noted in the Arminian controversy, occurred at the universities, control of which was jealously guarded by the magistracy. The magistrates who were determined to keep the church national (*Volkskerk*), pursued a policy of tolerance in doctrinal matters. They refused to make subscription to the Canons of Dort mandatory for professors appointed at the state universities. Moreover, the Church Order of Dort, which would have guaranteed orthodoxy in doctrine and practice (discipline) in the established church, was rejected by the magistracy. In its desire to keep the church subordinate to the state (the magistracy feared clerical domination in secular affairs), the States General forbade the calling of any national synods after Dordrecht and thus greatly limited the unity and organization of the church. Increasingly the powerful magistracy revealed non-orthodox, liberal tendencies. This was all the more dangerous because public officials were expected to be members of the established church, although membership was not mandatory. Thus establishment encouraged nominal membership in the church and greatly hampered the exercise of discipline.

Nevertheless, the prestige and influence of the Reformed churches in the seventeenth century was impressive. Although freedom of religion and speech was granted to all in the Dutch Republic (a fact which encouraged religious and political refugees to emigrate to Holland in large numbers), the public practice of religion was denied to all but the Reformed churches. Dissenters and Roman Catholics worshipped privately and inconspicuously. Not only did the established church enjoy the exclusive privilege of public worship, but it was also financed from the public treasury. The Reformed churches, therefore, enjoyed a favored position, and it should be added that in the first century of its existence the church exploited these opportunities to the fullest degree. Its leadership was dynamic and devoted, and the policy of evangelization was seriously and successfully pursued. By 1650 approximately one-half of the populace had membership in the Netherlands Reformed Church.

The florescence of Dutch Calvinism in the seventeenth century coincides with a truly phenomenal flourishing of the arts and sciences. The Golden Age is a period of unprecedented material, technological, scientific, and cultural progress. To be sure, this development cannot be attributed exclusively to the influence of Calvinism, but it is true that the Reformed faith initially encouraged an attitude toward the world which stands in sharp contrast to the other-worldliness of medieval Catholicism. Although Calvinists taught that man was *passive* in regeneration, they also affirmed that the reborn Christian should be *active* in God's world. Although special grace was the free gift of God to lost sinners, the elect were called to live a life to the honor and glory of God. In Calvinist theology divine sovereignty was opposed to human autonomy, but the redeemed and liberated Christian was called to exercise his freedom in this world, for God is sovereign over all of life. In stressing the priority of the religious aspect of life, Calvinists also affirmed the importance and the relevance of the faith to all life. The result was a new orientation toward the world, one in which religion and life were not separated but united. All of life had significance and every calling was for the Christian a divinely given vocation. By its emphasis upon the nobility of labor, Calvinism contributed to the development of Christian character; it encouraged the development of such traits as sobriety, diligence, thrift, orderliness, and ingenuity. The world, though corrupted by sin, remained the place of the Christian's activities. Thus the Calvinistic life and world view could and did support and encourage cultural activities on a wide scale. Dutch Calvinists could enthusiastically participate in the mighty cultural achievements of the age in the areas of commerce and navigation, exploration and colonization, land reclamation and building, science and learning, art and philanthropy. Unfortunately, this period of the florescence of both Dutch Calvinism and the Dutch Republic was comparatively short, for by the end of the seventeenth century there began a gradual decline in the fortunes of both church and state.

The Decline of Dutch Calvinism

Among the factors which contributed to the decline of Dutch Calvinism one of the most important was doubtless the close relationship of church and state. The church was subject to the control of the state at crucial points. No national synods could be called without state concurrence, and that was not forthcoming. The fact that the *Hervormde Kerk* was a national church made membership in it desirable and respectable, but the church could exercise little control over its members. Consequently, the church was plagued increasingly with the problem of nominal membership.

State control of the universities did not aid the cause of orthodox Calvinism. In the course of the seventeeth and eighteenth centuries these institutions where Reformed clergymen were trained became more and more influenced by rationalism. At the universities the influence of such thinkers as Descartes, Bayle, and Spinoza was considerable. Theology, which was regarded as the queen of the sciences when the universities were founded, gradually became divorced from the sciences. Even in the department of theology the rationalistic, analytical, critical method of Descartes found supporters. The approach of strict orthodox theologians, however, tended to be dogmatic and authoritarian. These differences in approach led to conflict between the theologians Coccejus and Voetius. Whereas Voetius demanded that in the development of Reformed theology the Scriptures should be viewed in accordance with the accepted creeds, Coccejus favored an "unbiased," critical examination of the Bible in order to discover its truths. Quite obviously, this latter, individualistic view, however dynamic, poses a constant threat to the validity of the creeds, and as such it was, and is, anathema to orthodoxy. This controversy was but one of several which arose within the church. Others concerned the problem of Sabbath observance, the covenantal unity of Old and New Testaments, the body-soul relationship, the question of original sin, and the eternal generation of Christ. These several disputes did not serve to enhance the position of the church, but rather fostered strife, divisiveness, and doubt. The public agitation produced by these conflicts was at times so great that the state forbade further discussion and debate about the issues involved.

Rationalism in the theological schools was in turn reflected in the pulpit. During the eighteenth century theological liberalism greatly increased in the churches. Frequently sermons were not the proclamation of the gospel, but learned discourses on Biblical and ethical subjects.

In reaction to rationalistic theology in the pulpit, there developed among orthodox believers a strong experiential, mystical, pietistic emphasis in religion. Orthodox Calvinists also became more and more anti-cultural in their outlook. The uneducated, humble believers of the lower classes were offended by the worldly life of the educated, sophisticated, wealthy church members. During the course of the eighteenth century, class differences tended to reflect religious differences. The division between uneducated and educated, poor and wealthy, became increasingly a gulf between the orthodox and the liberals or even libertines. Calvinism as a theology, not as a life and world view, remained alive among the common people even when liberalism predominated among the clergy and upper classes.

In the absence of orthodox preaching in the pulpit, orthodox believers sought to strengthen their faith in conventicles, religious meetings held in the homes of Christians and led by lay teachers. The lay exhorter again became an important person in the nurturing of spiritual life. The Dutch conventicle movement was influenced also by German Pietism and English Methodism. One of the most popular religious books of the eighteenth century was Bunyan's *Pilgrim's Progress*. These conventicle Calvinists adhered to the Canons of Dort and strongly emphasized both human depravity and divine election. The rigid, exclusive emphasis upon these two doctrines produced a one-sidedly introspective religion which was forever probing the depths of depravity and seeking signs or evidences of election. Since the wrath of God over sin was stressed rather than His love for the sinner, the dominant religious motif frequently became that of abject self-negation and despairing hope. For these Calvinists the world and human nature were evil; they cultivated a Protestant type of asceticism which was both rigorous and depressing. Still, it was in the conventicles (*Gezelschappen*) that the faithful, orthodox believers met, experienced the fellowship of the saints, and professed their belief in the cardinal truths of the Reformed faith. Thus these humble believers preserved and passed on to posterity the Calvinistic heritage which was largely lost in the Netherlands Reformed Church during the eighteenth century.

The influence of Calvinism in church and state was gradually diminishing. At the same time that Calvinism was becoming ever more anti-cultural, the intelligentsia and elite were increasingly receptive to French culture. Among the polite upper classes the French language was spoken, French manners and morals imitated. Liberal Dutchmen embraced the social, religious, and political ideals of the French Enlightenment, though not in their most radical deistic and atheistic forms. The outbreak of the French Revolution was hailed by Dutch liberals as ushering in a new period of political enlightenment, tolerance, and democracy. A large segment of the Dutch populace became hostile to the House of Orange and welcomed the invasion of the Netherlands by French forces in 1795. As a result of this invasion the Dutch Stadtholder was compelled to go into exile. A new state, the Batavian Republic, was established on the ideals of the French Revolution: fraternity, equality, liberty, and the sovereignty of the people. The establishment of the Batavian Republic at once rendered the position of the Netherlands Reformed Church problematic. The idea of an established Calvinistic church was in radical conflict with the equalitarian ideals of the revolution. Consequently, the connections between church and state were severed already in 1796. Although this arrangement was not a permanent one, the Reformed churches were in serious trouble, because state financial support was no longer assured. A serious economic depression in the first decade of the eighteenth century intensified the financial crisis in the established church. Payment of ministers' salaries was irregular, sometimes deferred, and even cancelled. Nor was the church, which had leaned upon the state for financial support for more than two centuries, now able to become self-supporting. The church seemed unable to continue without state aid. Consequently, the efforts of churchmen and people were directed toward the re-establishment of the *national* church.

The Christian character of the public school was likewise threatened by the new political ideals. The Batavian Republic did not regard its task to be that of protecting and supporting a particular religious group, but rather that of encouraging and cultivating morals among *all* the people, so that they might be good citizens. The school was to serve the common good by educating for citizenship; it was to prepare men for the pursuit of individual happiness, a good and useful life. Accordingly, only the most universal religious ideals were to be inculcated at the schools and all that was particularistic or sectarian was to be avoided. These ideals continued to dominate the liberal attitude toward public education after the fall of the Batavian Republic in 1813, and they constituted one of the greatest threats to the continued existence of Dutch Calvinism.

French domination of the Netherlands continued only as long as Napoleon was triumphant. With the major defeat of Napoleon in 1813, the French authority collapsed, and the Netherlands regained political independence. The Stadtholder was recalled and made the head of a constitutional monarchy. The end of French rule, however, by no means meant the end of French influence, for in the new government French reforms, penal codes, and political ideology persisted.

One of the major problems confronting the new government was settlement of the knotty problem of the relationship between church and state. The financial problem of the church was solved when the Reformed Church once again became the established church, but now other problems, both ecclesiastical and dogmatic in character, were to plague the church. The status and organization of the Netherlands Reformed Church was now determined by the *state,* and a new church order was formulated by the Ministry of Internal Affairs. This order abolished the presbyterian pattern of church government (destroying the local autonomy of the congregation) and introduced a centralized, administrative, synodical system. The democratic character of the church was changed to one that was autocratic, control of the church from congregational level to synod being vested in administrative bodies which were responsible to the government (king).

Nominally, the state was concerned only with the administrative, organizational affairs of the church. The general synod or ruling body of the church determined the membership of provincial synods, classes, and consistories; it determined the size of congregations and administered the finances and charities of the church. In this centralized system the local congregation was no longer regarded as an autonomous unit under the jurisdiction of the local consistory. Instead, the local church was considered a branch of the national church.

Worse still, the central ruling body determined the doctrinal position of the church. It refused to recognize the Canons of Dort as one of the original creedal statements of the *Hervormde Kerk*. The state-controlled synodical system was intended to keep the church a *national* institution in which orthodox and liberal views of Christianity could exist side by side. Thus the Belgic Confession and the Heidelberg Catechism were retained as creedal formularies in the church, and candidates for the ministry were compelled to subscribe to them. At the same time, however, the concept of doctrinal freedom (*leervrijheid*) was guaranteed by a weasel-worded formulation of the subscription formula. The candidate promised "in good faith to accept and heartily believe *the doctrine which is contained in the adopted forms of unity which agree with the Word of God*." The clause "which agree with the Word of God" was sufficiently ambiguous to allow the candidate to interpret *which* doctrines in the creed were, in his judgment, in agreement with the Bible. Thus the ministers of the church could interpret their subscription to the creeds in either an orthodox or liberal manner. Consequently the national church had ministers who were orthodox and those who were liberal in the same pulpit. This synodical system was a repudiation of the orthodox Calvinist concept of the church, and it constituted a serious threat to the Reformed character of the national church. The principle of establishment, to which the Reformed churches owed so much in their formative stages, proved in the end to be disastrous to the idea of a pure, Calvinistic church.

The Rebirth of Dutch Calvinism

In the nineteenth century Reformed Christians in the established church were engaged in a battle for existence. The history of Dutch Calvinism in this century is a struggle to break with the state-dominated synodical system (that is, an attempt to restore control of the ecclesiastical organization to the church), to restore the national church to its confessional basis (as determined in 1618 at Dordrecht), to restore the Christian (Reformed) character of the public school, in short, to re-establish the church as the soul or conscience of a Christian nation.

Various methods were pursued in the attempt to achieve these objectives. There was first of all the individual protest against abuses in the established church. Important documents of protest are: Schotsman's *Eerezuil Voor Dordt* (1819), a defense of the Canons; Da Costa's *Bezwaren Tegen Den Geest Der Eeuw* (1823), a vigorous, militant protest against the preponderance of enlightenment ideas in church, education, politics and other areas; and D. Molenaar's *Adres aan alle mijne Hervormde Geloofsgenooten* (1827) which called for a national synod, the restoration of the Reformed creeds, and a revision of the subscription formulary. These protests stirred up much bitter controversy, but they failed to achieve the desired end. The great majority of the educated upper classes (the voters) was too enlightened to take seriously the protests of the narrow, strict Calvinists, who were accused, moreover, of disturbing the peace of church and state.

Another method pursued was that of petitioning the Synod to restore the authority of the creeds in the church. Such petitions, bearing the signatures of clergy and church members, also went unheeded. The synod, as an administrative body, simply asserted that it had no jurisdiction in the interpretation of the creeds, since this was a purely theological matter! The problem of interpreting the creeds was viewed as a personal matter, a question of the individual conscience. Indeed, the synod could not impose a doctrinal interpretation upon the members of the *national* church in which *all* Reformed (that is, non-Catholic, non-Lutheran, non-Anabaptist) Christians had a place. Since the national church had no synod, and its clergy was predominantly liberal, the so-called strict Calvinists (mostly common people) were helpless and could only protest against the existing situation.

Still a third attempt to reform the national church was the establishment of "Societies of Christian Friends." These societies were formed to revive interest in the Reformed faith within local churches, by individual and group evangelization. In this they were often successful and a new enthusiasm for Calvinism was engendered at local levels. Closely linked with this movement was the *Reveille,* a spiritual revival which found support especially among the upper classes, and contributed significantly to the rebirth of a revitalized Christianity there.

Finally, there was an attempt to gain reform in the church by means of the ballot. It was only as suffrage was gradually extended that this method had any chance of success. Not until 1867 did the churches regain their ecclesiastical rights. By a law of 1867 the local congregations again received the right to call their pastors. Once this had been achieved, consistories could control the local situation by calling orthodox pastors. These orthodox ministers could in turn make their influence felt within classes and provincial synods. Orthodoxy once again had a voice within the national church.

The objective of Calvinists during much of the nineteenth century was the restoration of the Netherlands as a Protestant, Calvinist state. Their aim was to restore orthodox Christianity *within* the national church and *within* the public school. The Dutch Republic, argued the Calvinist historian Groen van Prinsterer, had been established as a Christian nation, with a Reformed (Calvinistic) church and school. In his *History of the Fatherland* (*Geschiedenis des Vaderlands*) Groen defended the view that the Dutch state had flourished while it was Christian (Reformed), but had declined when the nation relinquished orthodox Christianity. The Netherlands nation, Groen pleaded, should *return* to its orthodox Christian basis. On this ground Dutch Calvinists in the nineteenth century sought to restore the Christian character of the public school. As we noted earlier, instruction in the public school had been put on a nonsectarian basis during the Batavian Republic. In the nineteenth century "liberal"

Christians (who still held to the name Reformed) desired a national school for all Dutch children, for Protestants, Catholics, and Jews alike. Such a national public school could only exist if there were freedom of religion and tolerance of all religious views. The liberals were so successful in championing their ideal of tolerance, that the Bible was banned from the public school. Indeed, the attempt to make of the public school a neutral institution went so far that textbooks were proofread by Jews, Catholics, and Protestants, each having the privilege of expunging from them anything hostile to his particular religious convictions. To such an absurd position the principle of tolerance led. This situation was, of course, intolerable both to Calvinists and Catholics.

Any attempt to restore the schools to a Reformed basis was doomed to failure in the enlightened, liberal climate of the nineteenth century. All petitions to restore the Bible to the school were simply rejected. Proponents of Christian education then sought to restore the Bible and Christianity to the schools by making religious instruction optional, but this attempt also failed because of "liberal" opposition. The only avenue left open to orthodox Christians and Catholics was the establishment of separate schools. But even here the orthodox encountered the opposition of liberal politicians. The idea of separate schools was resisted on the ground that the public school was a *national* institution and that education was the function of the *state,* not the parent. Only gradually, after much bitter struggle, did the idea of parentally controlled, separate Christian schools take hold. The entire cost of erecting the first "schools with the Bible" was borne by the parents, who, for the most part, belonged to the poorest working classes. For their zeal they gained, moreover, the ridicule and abuse of their fellow countrymen. But the principle which these pioneers of Christian education defended was triumphant in the end. The Christian schools (Protestant and Catholic) were in the twentieth century put on an equal footing with the public school, the cost of education being met almost entirely from the public treasury.

In the Netherlands today Christian education is available at all levels, from grammar school to university. The apex of this system of Protestant Christian education is the Free (Reformed) University of Amsterdam, founded in 1880. Thus the Christian school was indeed re-established, not now as a national or public school, but as a separate, parentally controlled, governmentally financed institution. Perhaps nothing was as important for the revitalization of Dutch Calvinism as this struggle for Christian education.

Dutch Calvinists, then, were compelled to relinquish their ideal of a national Christian (Reformed) school, but they did achieve the ideal of Christian education in separate schools. A similar process is evident in the attempt to restore the national church to its Reformed creedal basis. The establishment of an orthodox Reformed church could be attained only by schism, by secession from the national church.

The first secession from the state church was the direct result of violations of the state-imposed church order. In 1834 Rev. H. De Cock was censured and defrocked for having violated the church order by baptizing the infants of parents who were not members of his congregation. These parents did not wish to have their children baptized by a non-Reformed minister, for they took seriously and quite literally their Baptismal confession: "Do you acknowledge the doctrine which is contained in the Old and the New Testament, and in the articles of the Christian faith, and which is taught *here* in this Christian church to be the true and complete doctrine of salvation?" Since these parents could not disassociate the minister from the church, they demanded that an orthodox minister perform the rite, and this Rev. De Cock was willing to do, although he was fully aware of the violation of the church order involved. De Cock, who was converted to orthodox Christianity after he had become a minister, was an ardent and militant Calvinist. His publication of the Canons of Dort and his public attack upon liberal ministers in the church ("wolves in the sheepcote") did not endear him to his colleagues or to the synod. He was regarded as another of those rigid, narrow Calvinists who maliciously attacked the integrity of his fellow ministers. When De Cock deliberately violated the church order by baptizing infants not born within his congregation, and refused to apologize for his attack on fellow clergymen, he was regarded by the authorities as a schismatic who put individual views above the law of the church and thus threatened its good order and peace. Accordingly, De Cock was censured, then deposed, until he would acknowledge his error and abide by the church order.

DeCock's action was the signal for other orthodox ministers to protest the non-Reformed character of the church order to synod and king, but all to no avail. Failing to receive favorable action from the church government, a small number of ministers decided that they could not in good conscience remain members of the established church which, in their judgment, had become apostate. In 1834 they drew up an "Act of Departure and Return" by which separation from the state church became a reality. The Separatists (*Afgescheidenen*) departed from the established, "false church," to return to the *true* Reformed Church; the newly founded church was therefore designated the "Old Netherlands Reformed Church." Other ministers prominent in the small Separatist church were: H. P. Scholte, A. Brummelkamp, S. Van Velzen, A. C. Van Raalte, and G. F. Gezelle Meerburg.

The establishing of a rival Reformed Church did not meet with the approval of the national church or government. The Separatists' claim to the name "Reformed" and to the church properties was promptly rejected. Since the Separatists were not legally recognized as a church, but were regarded as sectarians, they were denied the use of church properties and income. Indeed, they were forbidden to assemble for public worship and celebration of the sacraments. In order to frustrate the attempts of the Separatists to meet for worship in private homes, the government conveniently enforced a provision of the Napoleonic code which forbade all assemblies of twenty people or more without governmental permission. Since the Separatists insisted on using the name "Reformed" and claimed to be the "Old True Reformed Church," they could hardly seek governmental approval for their meetings, and still less could they expect to receive its sanction of them. The constitution of the Netherlands did guarantee freedom of religion, but no church (assembly) was permissible without governmental approval. Thus the Separatists were left with two alternatives: either to assemble in private homes with less than twenty people, or to violate the penal code by way of protest. For violating the law the Separatists were repeatedly fined, maltreated, and imprisoned. Governmental recognition was finally gained, but only after the Separatists had endured much vilification and persecution.

In 1847 a group of these courageous Calvinists became convinced that their ideals of establishing a true Reformed church and Christian schools could not be realized in their homeland. Accordingly, they considered the possibility of emigrating to another part of the globe where they might enjoy genuine freedom of religion. A severe economic crisis (potato crop failure in 1845) strengthened them in their resolve. Under the leadership of the Reverends Van Raalte and Scholte these Calvinists reluctantly left their native land to seek in midwest America, in Holland, Michigan, and in Pella, Iowa, the freedom they so dearly valued. Another painful schism within the Van Raalte colony in 1857 led to the establishment of the Christian Reformed Church.

When the churches that remained in the Netherlands finally received governmental recognition, the secession became final. In 1854 the Separatists founded a theological school at Kampen. This seminary continues to this day to serve the Reformed churches in the training of candidates for the gospel ministry.

A second major secession from the established church followed in 1886, this time under the leadership of Dr. A. Kuyper. This extremely gifted man, minister, theologian, scholar, orator, journalist, professor, and politician, devoted his life to the revival of Dutch Calvinism, not merely as a theological system, but also as a life and world view, a leavening force in Dutch national life. Although he desired reform within the national church, Kuyper became convinced that this ideal could not be achieved in nineteenth-century Netherlands. Like De Cock, Kuyper became involved in a conflict with the ecclesiastical government of the church. His congregation, which was orthodox, refused to approve church membership for a group of young people who had been catechized by, and made profession of faith under, ministers who denied the deity of Christ. Kuyper and his consistory were deposed from office, and as a result of this conflict, Kuyper and a very large following withdrew from the established church in 1886.

This secession is known as the *Doleantie* ("sorrowing")

because the Calvinists sadly left the national church, having come to the realization that it was no longer truly Reformed. In 1892 the *Doleerende Kerken* merged with the churches of the *Afscheiding* (1834) and together they became the *Gereformeerde Kerken in Nederland.* These churches returned to the creedal basis of the early Dutch Calvinist church, the three forms of unity. Under the brilliant, inspiring leadership of men like Groen van Prinsterer, Abraham Kuyper and Herman Bavinck, there has followed a genuine rebirth of Dutch Calvinism. These leaders strove to remove the anti-cultural tendencies which had developed among Reformed people in preceding centuries. They labored mightily to restore and renew the cultural perspective of Reformed Christianity.

In conclusion, we briefly call attention to the role of Groen van Prinsterer and Abraham Kuyper in the revitalization of Dutch Calvinism. Groen, prominent historian and statesman, sought to arouse the Calvinist consciousness of the nation in his publications *History of the Fatherland* and *Unbelief and Revolution* (*Ongeloof en Revolutie*). Groen protested vigorously against the ideals of the French revolution which had been espoused in the Netherlands. The sovereignty of the people he regarded as tyrannical and a real threat to individual liberty. To it he opposed the sovereignty of God, whose will, for political life, is to be found in the Scriptures. Groen called for a political program based on principles, the principles of God's Word. It was the aim of Groen to recall the Dutch people to their origins as a Calvinist nation. As a member of the Chamber of Deputies, Groen defended the Christian school movement and demanded that the state provide for public Christian education. Although Groen's attempts to achieve reform of the national schools failed, his efforts (and those of others) did result in the establishment of Christian schools on a Reformed basis.

Similarly, Groen's attempt to re-establish the Netherlands as a Christian (Calvinist) state was doomed to failure, for the Calvinists were now a minority group within a democratic state. Thus the Calvinists were compelled either to exert their influence within existing political parties or to begin a separate political organization of their own. The conflict of principles between liberals and Calvinists (in the school struggle, for example) allowed of no compromise, as we have seen. Therefore the Calvinists, in 1878, established the Anti-Revolutionary Party in order to pursue political objectives in accordance with Biblical principles. Through their party organization the Calvinists were able to engage in the struggle for Christian schools more effectively. In their political program, the Calvinists constantly emphasized underlying principles, compelling their opponents to consider and weigh these also. Subsequently, Groen's ideal of political action based upon a program of principles was adopted by all Dutch political parties. Roman Catholics, Liberals, and Socialites today campaign on a program of principles. And thus Dutch Calvinists have been able to witness to their principles and also have found the means of practicing them, at least partially, through Christian political action.

Groen's friend and successor, Abraham Kuyper, vigorously pursued the policy of revitalizing Dutch Calvinism. Kuyper was not only the theorist of Neo-Calvinism, but also its dynamic leader. He labored to make the ordinary church members conscious of their task as Christians *in* the world and *within* the nation. An able journalist, Kuyper was for many years the editor of *De Standaard,* a Christian newspaper which sought to acquaint the uneducated Christian with the issues of the day. In 1874 Kuyper was elected to the Chamber of Deputies, where he continued the battle for "free" schools and a "free" church, that is, free from governmental control and supervision. The principles for Christian political action Kuyper laid down in his book *Ons Program.* He became the first leader of the Anti-Revolutionary Party. It was Kuyper who in 1886 led half a million Calvinists out of the established church when it proved impossible to restore this church to a Calvinist creedal basis (Canons of Dort) with autonomy in ecclesiastical affairs. Kuyper also led the movement which resulted in the establishment of the Free University in 1880.

The leadership of this great Calvinist is well summarized in the following statement:

> Kuyper appealed to the "small people" not to tolerate the "ecclesiastical and political tyranny of a privileged obligarchy," by which he meant the prosperous burgher class. Through masterful leadership he worked up an

> enthusiasm which in a few years made him the most prominent political figure in the country. He completely transformed the small intellectual group organized by Groen into a mass movement with slogans, popular campaigns, and party publications. His ideal was a total rebirth. Not only the political dominance of the Liberals, but also their intellectual monopoly was to be broken. Kuyper demonstrated the power of democracy when, with donations from the poor, he founded a university to give his co-religionists intellectual and spiritual leaders. The money was collected in scores of thousands of small gifts, a few guilders, a few dimes, sometimes a few cents. Many universities have been endowed by millionaires who have hardly missed the millions they bestowed on their foundations. Very few owe their existence, as did Kuyper's foundation, to the masses.[13]

Under the leadership of Kuyper, Calvinism again became a significant force in the Netherlands. Separate Christian schools were established, a university founded, a Christian political program inaugurated, Christian periodicals and dailies published. The aim of the Anti-Revolutionary Party "to raise the forgotten and so-called backward part of the Netherlands to an integrated scientific, religious, and social consciousness" was largely realized. And this program, initiated by Kuyper, has been carried on ever more extensively in the twentieth century.

The revival of a dynamic Neo-Calvinism in the liberal cultural climate of nineteenth century Netherlands was possible only through schism and separation. Calvinists who believed in the ideal of a truly Reformed church, pure in doctrine and practice, and a genuinely Reformed life and world view, had no alternative but to withdraw from the existing national church and school. Kuyper saw that the ideal of a *national* Christian (Reformed) church and school could no longer be sought or realized within the framework of the non-Christian, secular state. Nevertheless, the Neo-Calvinists were aware of their responsibility to strive for the revitalization of Christianity within the nation, and their most immediate, practical, and effective method was that of the

13. Bernard H. M. Vlekke, *Evolution of the Dutch Nation,* p. 317.

separate, Christian organization. In the twentieth century the principle of separate Christian organization has been extended to every area of life by the Neo-Calvinists. Although there has been increasing criticism of this Christian separatism in the post war years, the fact remains that the many Christian organizations attest to a strong theological consciousness and a genuine desire to profess and practice Christian principles in a non-Christian world.

Large numbers of Dutch Calvinists did not go along with the Neo-Calvinism of Kuyper, but remained instead within the established, national church. There they have continued their witness, seeking, without the benefit of separate organizations, to call the nation back to Christianity. Their ideal continues to be that of the national church (*Volkskerk*). Developments within the national church in recent years, the severance of ties with the state, the revival of orthodoxy, attest to the fact that their efforts and sacrifices have not been in vain.

Thus the Reformed faith, which providentially became the predominant Protestant manifestation of Christianity in the Netherlands, and which has had a unique, continuous development there during four long, troubled centuries, remains a virile, vital, dynamic Christianity. The Calvinist tradition, based upon the authority of the Holy Scriptures, creedally defined in the forms of unity, and acknowledging the sovereignty of God in every area of life, is once again a significant force in Dutch national life. Whereas the impact of Calvinism in America has become minimal, Dutch Calvinism continues to contribute to national culture. To use a Dutch expression: *De Gereformeerden tellen mee,* that is, the Reformed people count; they are, and have been, to a greater or lesser degree, theologically and culturally significant over a period of four centuries. Under divine guidance, Calvinism has played a greater role in the Netherlands than in any other country on the globe. The continued existence and witness of Calvinists within the national church and in the independent Reformed churches testifies to the grace of God working in the lives of His erring but redeemed people, and thus the Calvinists continue to be a blessing to the Netherlands nation.

BIBLIOGRAPHY

Brillenburg-Wurth, G., *De Antithese in Dezen Tijd,* Kampen, 1940.

——————, *Het Calvinisme Vandaag,* Wageningen, n. d.

Dankbaar, W. F., *Hoogtepunten uit het Nederlandsche Calvinisme in de Zestiende Eeuw,* Haarlem, 1946.

Kluit, M. E., *Het Reveil in Nederland,* Amsterdam, 1936.

Knappert, L., *Het Ontstaan en de Vestiging van het Protestantisme in de Nederlanden,* Oosthoek, 1924.

——————, *Geschiedenis der Hervormde Kerk onder de Republiek en het Koninkrijk der Nederlanden,* 2 vols., Amsterdam, 1910-1911.

Kromminga, D. H., *The Christian Reformed Tradition,* Grand Rapids, 1943.

Nauta, D., *Het Calvinisme in Nederland,* Franeker, 1949.

Nobbs, Douglas, *Theocracy and Toleration,* Cambridge, 1938.

Reitsma, Johannes, *Geschiedenis van de Hervorming en de Hervormde Kerk der Nederlanden,* 4th ed., ed. by J. Lindeboom, Utrecht, 1916.

Rullman, J. C., *De Afscheiding in de Nederlandsch Hervormde Kerk der XIXe Eeuw,* 4th ed., Kampen, 1930.

——————, *De Doleantie in de Nederlandsch Hervormde Kerk der XIXe Eeuw,* 3d ed., Kampen, 1929.

Uit Den Bogaard, M. Th., *De Gereformeerden en Oranje Tijdens het Eerste Stadhouderloze Tijdperk,* Groningen, 1955.

Van Ruler, A. A., *Kuypers Idee eener Christelijke Cultuur,* Nijkerk, 1937.

Van Schelven, A. A., *Uit den Strijd der Geesten,* Amsterdam, 1944.

Vlekke, B. H. M., *Evolution of the Dutch Nation,* New York, 1945.

Waterink, J., *et al., Cultuurgeschiedenis van het Christendom,* Vols. III, IV, V; Amsterdam, 1950-1951

4

THE HISTORY AND DEVELOPMENT OF CALVINISM IN SCOTLAND AND ENGLAND

Scotland

Beginnings

Before 1550 Scotland was a Roman Catholic country, as were all the lands of Western Europe. Scotland was poor and backward, and within her hilly borders human behavior left much to be desired. Throughout the middle ages there had been hosts of small wars between the many clans, and rather major wars with the English to the south. Economically, the people were poor: peasants were mistreated by the nobles; parishioners were burdened in general by the clergy.

About 1525 a young noble, Patrick Hamilton, advocated a more evangelical type of faith, and for his views and utterances he was burned at the stake. Hamilton's martyrdom was followed in 1546 by that of George Wishart, who had worked hard for an inside reformation of the Roman Church. Before he was killed he translated the First Helvetic (Swiss) Confession into the Scottish language.

It was Wishart's disciple, John Knox, who effected the launching of the Protestant churches. Knox was not profound, but he was courageous. He was not a first-class theologian, but he was an able organizer. It was he who piloted the Scottish Reformation through the intricacies of hostile foreign diplomacy and English antagonism. In 1560 the Scottish Estates (Parliament) repudiated Catholicism as the state religion and approved a Protestant confession of faith. In general the Scottish Reformation was bloodless, and for all practical purposes it witnessed the disappearance of Romanism from this land of hills and clouds. The basic character of the Scottish Reformation is indicated in the following manifestations: (1) a non-hierarchical ministry; (2) the institutional character of preaching; (3) careful discipline in and by the church.

The founders of Protestantism in Scotland claimed to be reformers in their own right before they were Calvinists. One of their number said that they "took not their pattern from any Kirk in the world, no, not from Geneva itself." But whether these strong men admitted it or not, Calvin's *Institutes* permeated the early confessional statements. After Knox's death the churches became clearly Presbyterian in their government, declaring for the equality of all ministers. This fact almost belies the foregoing assertion of the founders.

Difficulties

Much of the difficulty experienced by Scottish Calvinism comes from the friction between two views or ideas — the one being that the Bible is the sole authority for the church, and the other being that the government as the protector of the church has something to say in its affairs. The seventeenth century is a story of conflict between these two ideas. The view that the church is not to be trampled on by the state prevailed, but unfortunately the church did not take the logical step of refusing state subsidy. The minds of Scottish Calvinists did not see that a church and its clergy can be entirely free from political pressure only if state funds and endowments are refused.

The 1600s were also difficult for Scottish Calvinism because the country had to fight off English encroachment, the English, until about 1648, being very eager to establish their own reformation (Anglicanism) on Scottish soil. This threat did not cease entirely until after 1689, when England and Scotland both received William and Mary as the new monarchs imported from Calvinistic Netherlands. In 1707 a formal union which recognized Scotland's preferences for a Presbyterian state church was effected between England and Scotland.

The eighteenth century, too, was a difficult time, because of differences in thought within the church. The intellectuals in the Calvinistic state universities, as well as many of the pastors of the churches, developed a theological point of view known as Moderatism. It was similar to the liberalism or modernism of our own day in that it allowed intellectual objections to weaken some of the hard-to-understand teachings of Calvinism, e.g., the doctrine of reprobation and the belief in the damnation of dying infants of non believing parents. Moderatism stressed the importance of personal behavior over conviction about doctrines, and it admitted to some uncertainty about the nature and person of God. It permitted latitude in one's personal beliefs, and it questioned the divine character of some Biblical passages. All this was most unfortunate and hard to cope with, because it originated with the better minds of the church. But there was reaction to it in the form of Evangelicalism. The tensions between these two groups in the Church of Scotland were never completely resolved. There were many major and tedious heresy trials, accompanied by name calling, but no unifying results.

Along with such grave difficulties there was the problem of patronage and its evils. Patronage was the relationship of a wealthy parishioner to a congregation whereby, in return for financial support and care of that church, this patron had the right to select the pastor. With the coming of Moderatism many of the patrons tended to select the bright young theological Liberals as they graduated from the universities — men who were unsatisfactory to the humble, orthodox laymen in the little churches. Protest as the orthodox might, church practice was on the side of the noble or wealthy man. Only the passage of decades eased this problem.

Decline and Disruption

The story of Calvinism in Scotland is a story of decline. It remained alive only in the confessions or standards which had been written in the 1500s and superseded by the Westminster Confession (London) of 1647. The "pulse of religious life was weak, and the tone of morality was low." "Vice, profanity, blasphemy, and grossness of every kind stalked . . . unabashed." "Even the most cultured were in the ranks of the coarse and scurrilous, and ministers of religion found delight in the rehearsal of untranslatable obscenity." Calvinism had failed to maintain morality in a land where it had a monopoly.

Alcoholism worsened; disparities in wealth widened; poverty deepened; and the church did not eradicate the tendency to be indebted to the aristocracy. Reverence for the Sabbath broke down, though this could be blamed conveniently on the influx of hundreds of Roman Catholics from Ireland.

To be sure, the evangelical wing of the church protested and resisted, but the ponderous machinery of the state church, the Church of Scotland, overrode attempts in the assemblies to rectify conditions. Something drastic had to happen. It did in the Disruption of 1843.

The Disruption was the exodus of some 451 Church of Scotland ministers with their congregations. The leader was Thomas Chalmers, and the name these seceders gave themselves was the Free Church of Scotland. This movement was a shattering blow to the smugness and prestige of the old church which claimed John Knox as its father. The Free Church came out with a new and clear witness; it revived historic Calvinism, both in the lives of individuals as well as in preaching and discipline. It added to itself several other fragments or splinters, which mergers or unions culminated in 1900 in the creation of the United Free Church of Scotland. A number of Free congregations, however, refrained from going along in this merger and they have come to be known as the "Wee Frees."

Today

Capping this complicated story came the union or reunion of the United Free Church with the old and original state church (Church of Scotland) about 1930. Thus most of the larger denominations are now back under one roof as one large and disestablished church. Today the relationship to the government is only a formal one. There remain many small evangelical churches as well as independent Presbyterian groups, but the bulk of that minority of Scotsmen who still attend church at all are in the reunited church of 1930.

Looking over the voluminous literature on Scottish Calvinism, one gets the impression that too much energy was sapped from the people by theological discussions and controversies — matters which could better have been taken care of by the clergymen and professional theologians. Furthermore, it seems that too much thinking went into the problem of church versus state, and not enough into ways and means to inculcate Christian morality in Scottish life and society. Scottish history shows that society can degenerate even though the landscape is studded with orthodox churches. The church was financially independent; it had things too easy. Today Scotland is only nominally Calvinistic. The vast majority of its folk pass the churches by. Unless there is a massive revival, with permanent momentum built into it, the only deposit of Calvinism in Scotland will be some very lovely devotional literature along with the many religious quaintnesses and the pithy sayings of these serious and sober people.

England

Beginnings

The beginnings of English Calvinism and its churches are very complicated and obscure. It is the story of a minority church which had to live in the shadow of a not-too-friendly, powerful state church, the so-called Established or Anglican church.

England became a Protestant country during the regime of Henry VIII in the 1530s. Henry understood something of theology, but his motives for separating his country from the papacy were, as everybody knows, not primarily theological. Thus it was that his own state church, the Anglican church, came into being without a clearly stated or characteristic theological basis of its own.

It was into this vacuum that a bit of Calvinistic thinking was allowed to trickle. Theologians can detect it in the Thirty-Nine Articles which became the confession of the Anglican church and in British thought and attitudes over the centuries, particularly in British respect for law and order. Calvinism entered England also in the form of churches. They were Presbyterian churches whose theology came out of Scotland, where Presbyterianism was the "law of the land." But from the very beginning of the Reformation in England, these Presbyterians were only a small minority who had to live under the threat of oppression, as did their cousins, the Puritans (Independents, Congregationalists, Brownists or Separatists).

Character

One of the founders and organizers of English Presbyterianism was Thomas Cartwright. As a teacher at Cambridge, he advanced six propositions (c. 1570) which gave the Calvinistic groups their protesting characteristic over against the state church. His propositions were: (1) Archbishops (as an office) should be abolished; (2) The offices should be limited to bishops who preach and to deacons who care for the poor (as in the apostolic church); (3) Every congregation should be governed by its own minister and presbyters (elders); (4) Ministers ought to be related to individual congregations and not be at large without specific or individual congregations for which they are responsible and to which they are answerable; (5) No man should be allowed to solicit to become a minister; (6) Ministers ought not to be ordained solely by bishops but openly and fairly by congregations after being chosen by the parishioners. Here was Presbyterianism crystal clear. For obvious reasons it was repugnant to Anglicanism, which retained something of the hierarchical organization of the Roman church.

The first Presbyterian congregation appeared near London (Wandsworth) in 1572. It was not really a full-fledged church but rather an association of individuals who perhaps retained their membership in the Anglican state church. There are no internal records of this little venture; but eventually there were scores of such cells throughout England. All copied the structure and order of Wandsworth.

The Westminster Confession

Between 1558 and 1625 England was ruled by Elizabeth Tudor and James Stuart. Both were hostile to Presbyterians: Elizabeth because she wanted religious uniformity throughout the land, and James I because he was an absolutist inflated by conceit. (He is the man who was called the wisest fool in Christendom.) Under these two monarchs, as well as under Charles I (1625-1649), Presbyterians had to lie low. But when the Civil War came in the 1640s, they asserted themselves in cooperation with the Puritans and Independents of the Anglican communion. It was during these years of war that there convened the famous Westminster Assembly (1643-1647), attended by Calvinists not only from England, but from Scotland and the Netherlands as well. The assembly was semi-official, having been summoned by Parliament itself. The intention was to revise or rewrite the Thirty-Nine Articles in order to make them Presbyterian in texture. But after a few months of work this was found to be almost impossible, and the effort was discontinued. Thus came the Westminster Confession, probably Calvinism's finest, and with it the two lovely catechisms, the Larger and the Shorter. Parliament approved these documents at the time, but because it shortly became Puritan and then reverted to Anglicanism (1660), the Westminster Confession was not widely nor permanently received by the English populace and clergy. Most Englishmen did not like Calvinism; to them it was a Scottish commodity.

Decline

In 1689 England imported from the Netherlands a new royal family in the persons of William III of Orange, and Mary. Immediately upon their accession to the throne toleration was accorded all Protestants. What motivated William was not, however, his own Calvinistic convictions — because they were weak — but political expediency. Regardless, however, of the motivation, the policy permitted Calvinism to breathe more freely.

The eighteenth century was a century of religious decay in England as it was in America, in Scotland, and in the Netherlands. In the case of British Calvinism the degeneration was due, humanly speaking, to neglect in requiring from the clergy oaths of doctrinal adherence. The basis of this neglect was the widely held belief that doctrinal standards as such were not God-inspired, and therefore not worthy of loyalty oaths. Another reason for decay was the low educational requirements for the clergy. Presbyterianism all but disappeared, most of it going the way of Unitarianism or Congregationalism.

But there was a revival during the nineteenth century. This came partly in the train of the Wesleyan or Methodist revival.

The Disruption of 1843 in the Scottish church and the emergence there of the Free Church made English Presbyterians more conscious of themselves and their weaknesses. In that state of mind these churches crossed into the twentieth century and have come down to our own age.

Summary

British Calvinism made two large contributions. The first is the Westminster Confession with its two catechisms. And the second is the steadying and catalyzing influence it had on the British social scene. The Westminster Confession is quite universally considered the most masterful of all confessions produced by Calvinists. It is said to be more profound, more philosophical, more logical, and more carefully symbolic than the Belgic Confession. And with reference to the second contribution, we suggest that partly owing to the Calvinism in its warp and woof, Britain is a land of law-abiding people, a land where there is little flagrant public disorder, few major crimes, some restraint on Sabbath desecration, and a deep respect for government and established authority. We like to believe that some of these attitudes or traits were embedded in the British tradition by the sturdy Presbyterians of bygone centuries.

Today Calvinism is weak in England. It is in evidence, but it is weak. So is Anglicanism. So is all religion. There is apathy, and lethargy, and pessimism about the future of the historic faiths and churches. The function of Christian mercy (care for the poor and down-trodden) has been taken over largely by an admirably organized government, leaving the church with the sole function of preaching redemption. This is a very difficult thing to do among a people whose traditions are Christian, and who do not regard themselves as pagan — people who love their churches in a way and have respect for God, but who do not care to attend their churches or voice their love. This refined apostasy is hard to reverse.

BIBLIOGRAPHY

Scotland

Andrews, William, (Ed.), *Bygone Church Life in Scotland,* London, 1899.

Barr, J., *The United Free Church of Scotland,* London, 1934.

Brown, T., *Annals of the Disruption,* Edinburgh, 1892.

Duke, John, *History of the Church of Scotland to the Reformation,* Edinburgh, 1937.

Edmunds, D. C., *The Early Scottish Church,* London, 1906.

Fleming, Arnold, *Huguenot Influences in Scotland,* Glasgow, 1953.

Henderson, H. F., *Religion in Scotland,* Paisley, 1920.

Henderson, H. F., *The Religious Controversies of Scotland,* Edinburgh, 1905.

Henderson, G. D., *Religious Life in Seventeenth Century Scotland,* Cambridge, 1937.

Macewen, A. R., *A History of the Church of Scotland,* London, 1913.

MacLeod, J., *Scottish Theology,* Edinburgh, 1943.

McNeill, J. T., *History and Character of Calvinism,* New York, 1954.

Mitchell, A., *Biographical Studies in Scottish Church History,* London, 1914.

Percy, Lord Eustace, *John Knox,* London, n. d.

Story, R. H., *The Apostolic Ministry in the Scottish Church,* Edinburgh, 1897.

Taylor, W. M., *The Scottish Pulpit from the Reformation to the Present Day,* New York, 1887.

Vos, Johannes G., *The Scottish Covenanters,* Philadelphia, 1940.

Walker, James, *The Theology and Theologians of Scotland,* Edinburgh, 1888.

England

Cragg, G. R., *Puritans in the Period of the Great Persecution, 1660-1688,* Cambridge, 1957.

Cremeans, C. D., *The Reception of Calvinistic Thought in England,* Urbana, Illinois, 1949.

Drysdale, A. H., *History of Presbyterianism in England,* London, 1889.

Haller, William, *Liberty and Reformation in the Puritan Revolution,* New York, 1955.

Haller, William, *The Rise of Puritanism, New York,* 1938.

Hopf, Constantin, *Martin Bucer and the English Reformation,* Oxford, 1946.

Hughes, Philip, *The Reformation in England,* London, 1950.

Hulbert, E. G., *The English Reformation and Puritanism,* Chicago, 1908.

Knappen, M. M., *Tudor Puritanism,* Chicago, 1939.

McNeill, J. T., *History and Character of Calvinism,* New York, 1954.

Martin, H., *Puritanism and Richard Baxter,* London, 1954.

Mitchell, A. F., *The Westminster Assembly,* Philadelphia, 1897.

Moffat, James, *The Presbyterian Churches,* London, 1928.

Ogilvie, H. J., *The Presbyterian Churches of Christendom,* London, 1925.

Reed, R. C., *History of the Presbyterian Churches of the World,* Philadelphia, 1917.

Tatham, G. B., *The Puritans in Power,* Cambridge, 1913.

Warfield, B. B., *The Westminster Assembly,* New York, 1931.

5

THE HISTORY AND DEVELOPMENT OF CALVINISM IN AMERICA

It has been observed rather frequently and with considerable warrant that God's special providence is clearly evident in the timing of the discovery of America. America was discovered just twenty-five years before Martin Luther inaugurated the Protestant Reformation. That religious upheaval which split the Roman Catholic establishment wide open and gave birth to the Protestant churches was to mean rigorous religious persecution. Exile or death was the dismal alternative for many thousands of Protestants. At this crucial juncture God opened up America as an asylum for the persecuted. Untold numbers saw clearly the hand of destiny and with economic, social, and political factors playing a not insignificant role, the new land was colonized. In these waves of emigration Calvinism was conveyed to America.

The Planting of Calvinism

There were five main emigrating streams that deposited Calvinism on this continent. The first in order of time and importance was the Pilgrim and Puritan which deposited its members in New England. The Pilgrims (Separatists or radical Puritans) under the leadership of John Robinson, a sturdy Calvinist who bested the Dutch Arminian Episcopius in debate during the Puritans' ten year stay in Holland, although appreciative of the refuge given them in the Low Countries, feared the loss of their distinctiveness. And when they experienced some economic difficulties and a renewal of the war between Holland and Spain loomed as a possibility, they decided to emigrate to America. They received a grant of land in Northern Virginia from the Virginia Company but contrary winds landed them on the bleak shores of New England in 1620. To circumvent the threat of anarchy and rebellion, since they possessed neither charter nor legal grant of land, they drew up on shipboard the Mayflower Compact, which was to serve as the basis of their government for many years. Elder William Brewster served as their first spiritual leader and William Bradford was the first governor of note. Growth was slow at first and hardships were many, but by 1643 the Plymouth colony boasted of ten towns and a population of twenty-five hundred. As Bradford's *History of Plymouth Plantation* and the extant sermons of that day indicate, doctrinally they were solidly Calvinistic.[1] As to church polity they were Congregational. That was inevitable since individual churches had severed themselves from the parent body in England and had resolved to go their own ways. Increase Mather wrote about them in 1677: "There never was such a generation that did so perfectly shake off the dust of Babylon, both as to civil and ecclesiastical constitution, as the first generation of Christians that came to this land for the gospel's sake."

The Puritans who left England eight years later, to the great relief of Charles I, were given a grant of land in New England, and under the leadership of John Endicott, who became the first governor, they settled in Salem in 1628. That colony, having a greater measure of royal favor and being less rigorous in its views, grew much more rapidly than its sister colony. By 1640 it numbered 20,000 colonists, most of them having come from the Cambridge area in England. They too were Calvinistic as to doctrine, and circumstances led them to the Congregational form of church government.

These Salem colonists had congenial contacts with the people in Plymouth. The help given by Dr. Samuel Fuller of the Plymouth colony to the Salem colony, when the latter was stricken by a severe epidemic, served to remove some

1. There are scholars who demur, it is true, but "if the beliefs of the Puritans [and Pilgrims] have not as a background such a genuinely Calvinistic theology as is commonly assumed without investigation, their theological conceptions are dominated by elements which, in spirit, must be described as typical of Calvinism, even if their genetic connection with the theology of Calvin is weak." G. Hammar, *Christian Realism in Contemporary American Theology,* p. 81.

of the prejudices that were harbored in Salem against Plymouth. Then when the need for a pastor and teacher in the Massachusetts Bay colony was urgent, on July 20, 1629, Francis Higginson and Samuel Skelton were questioned by the congregation (which had organized itself by covenant that spring), were approved by popular vote, and were ordained by imposition of hands of three or four elderly members of the church. Thus Congregationalism was born in the Bay Colony.[2] Other settlements followed suit and Congregationalism became accepted practice. When news of this action filtered back into England, there was considerable criticism, whereupon John Cotton of Boston, Richard Mather of Dorchester, John Davenport of New Haven, and Thomas Hooker of Connecticut collaborated in a defense of Congregationalism, published in 1646 and called the *Cambridge Platform.*[3] The Synod which convened in Cambridge in 1648 made this pronouncement as to doctrine and polity: "We do judge it [the Westminster Confession] to be very holy, judicious and orthodox in all matters of faith and we do freely and fully consent thereunto for the substance thereof. Only in those things which have respect unto church government and church discipline we refer ourselves to that platform agreed upon by the present assembly.[4]

2. Perry Miller insists, however, that it was due not to conspiring circumstances but to deliberate, venerable intention. "There is copious evidence," says he, "that though the leaders were careful not to advertise the fact, they were fully committed to putting into practice, the moment they set foot on shore, the Congregational rather than the Presbyterial order . . . . They had learned from a succession of English theologians (the greatest being William Ames) how to read the New Testament in a Congregational manner . . . . The *New England Way,* as it came to be called, was a fully developed blueprint in England which the Great Migration simply translated into an actual church." *The American Puritans,* p. 21.

3. Near the end of the seventeenth century and the beginning of the eighteenth, when liberalism began its invasion, Increase and Cotton Mather suggested the expedient of ministerial associations and conventions (somewhat resembling classes or presbyteries) in order to check it by scrupulous examination of candidates for the ministry. This plan was accepted in Connecticut (the Saybrook Platform of 1708), which veered towards Presbyterianism, but rejected in Massachusetts. In 1710 John Wise made another spirited defense of Congregationalism based on a philosophy of democracy.

4. William Hill, *American Presbyterianism,* p. 22.

In 1691 the Plymouth and Massachusetts Bay colonies were united. Congregationalism grew apace and by the outbreak of the Revolutionary War there were eight hundred Calvinistic Congregational churches in New England. As Gerstner observes, "New England, from the founding of Plymouth in 1620, to the end of the 18th century, was predominantly Calvinistic."[5]

The second emigrating stream bearing Calvinism to America was the *Dutch Reformed* (Reformed Church of America), which was responsible for the settlement of New York.

New Netherlands, later called New York, was established as a fur-trading colony in 1623 by the Dutch West Indies Company when thirty families were located in Ft. Nassau (Camden, N. J.) and Ft. Orange (Albany, N. Y.). In 1625 the population numbered two hundred.[6] In 1626 Peter Minuit, the first governor, bought Manhattan Island from the Indians at an incredible bargain.

In New Netherlands a dual religious arrangement, bound to be somewhat unsatisfactory, obtained whereby the minister, schoolmaster and sick visitors were appointed by Classis Amsterdam and received their salaries from the Dutch West Indies Company. In 1628 Jonas Michaelius, the first minister, arrived, celebrated communion and began to hold religious services. Thus the Calvinism of the Synod of Dort, with its Presbyterian form of church government (which is Calvinistic in origin), was instituted. Michaelius was succeeded by E. Bogardus, who found himself in constant conflict with the corrupt and incompetent governors Van Twiller (1633-1638) and Kieft (1638-1647). Under Bogardus's leadership a church edifice was erected, some of the money being pledged at a wedding reception where the wine flowed freely and the lightheaded pledged heavily.

Another factor impeding the free religious development of this colony was the "patroon system" initiated by the Dutch West Indies Company. Under this system anyone who brought over fifty families of emigrants within four years was

5. In *American Calvinism*, p. 16.

6. This colony never grew to large proportions because commercial interests remained very strong and because the population of Holland had been depleted by the war with Spain.

given a landed estate and titled a "patroon." The latter was obligated to provide one minister for the estate. Included among these landed-estate ministers was Megapolensis, who also worked among the Mohawks and holds the distinction of being the first Protestant missionary to the American Indians.[7]

Under Peter Stuyvesant, the last Dutch governor before the transition, trade flourished, population increased, and the "liberty of conscience" which obtained in the homeland (Holland was an asylum for the persecuted) was gradually introduced. That freedom of religion was continued when in 1644 the English forcibly wrested the colony from the Dutch and renamed it New York. A considerable number of persecuted French Huguenots and German Reformed from the Palatinate swelled the ranks, but Governor Dongan reported in 1687 that "the most prevailing opinion is that of the Dutch Calvinists."[8] By 1700 there were some twelve hundred Dutch Calvinist families in New York and by 1750 the number had grown to seventeen hundred. Religiously the colony proved to be quite static until it was enlivened by Frelinghuyzen and the Great Awakening.

The third stream, less considerable numerically but not in influence, was the *French Huguenot,* which deposited its representatives in the Middle and Southern Colonies.

Despite repressive measures, by the royalty for the most part and by many of the nobility, Protestantism had a fairly strong start in France. By the middle of the sixteenth century there was a large number of churches, served in the main by pastors trained in Geneva and consequently imbued with the doctrinal and church political views of Calvin. The first synod, comprising about fifty churches, met in Paris in 1559. It adopted a form of discipline, a confession of faith, and a modified Presbyterian form of church government. About this time the Protestants in France came to be called Huguenots[9]

7. He saved the life of the Jesuit missionary, Father Jogues, who was captured by the Mohawks and about to be tomahawked. Jogues wrote about the colony, "No religion is publicly exercised but the Calvinist and orders are to admit none but Calvinists." W. W. Sweet, *The Story of Religions in America,* p. 128.

8. Sweet, *op. cit.,* p. 135.

9. The derivation of the term is uncertain. The most plausible conjecture is the Swiss *Eidgenossen,* or confederates.

and the movement took on a political as well as a religious character. A series of struggles between Protestants and Roman Catholics followed, and these culminated in the savage massacre of seventy thousand Huguenots on St. Bartholomew's day in 1572. When Henry of Navarre took the throne in 1594 the country was weary of war. Under the influence of the Politiques, a patriotic group who favored toleration of religion in the interests of peace, Henry issued the Edict of Nantes on April 13, 1598. That edict permitted freedom of religion in some two hundred towns and in the castles of about three thousand nobles, and pledged immunity from interference in the church assemblies. In this period of toleration the Huguenots grew markedly in numbers and developed their educational institutions. After the assassination of Henry in 1610, however, a gradually increasing number of repressive measures was adopted. Church services were interrupted, synodical assemblies were prohibited, and when the irreligious Louis XIV ascended the throne in 1659 the last remaining vestiges of toleration were removed. He attempted the forcible "conversion" of the Huguenots to Roman Catholicism, and on the pretense that no Protestants remained in the land revoked in 1685 the Edict of Nantes. Despite prohibition of emigration and stationing of guards on the frontiers, some five hundred thousand of the best citizens of France emigrated to Prussia, England, Germany, and America.

Some of them settled in New York, when toleration was established there, and at first they were served by Dutch pastors who knew the French language. Others settled in Virginia and the Carolinas. They did not unite in a French Reformed Church but became members of the Dutch and German Reformed churches in the north and the Presbyterian churches in the south.

The fourth emigrating Calvinistic stream was the *German Reformed,* members of which settled for the most part in the Middle Colonies.

Germany, especially its Palatinate, was to serve as a haven of refuge for the persecuted Protestants of France. When news of the savage butchery of St. Bartholomew's Day reached him, Elector Frederick III sent a military force to assist the harried Huguenots and invite them to his domain. Many thousands accepted his offer. So, too, after the revocation of the Edict of Nantes. Twelve days after that fateful decision the Elector of Brandenburg issued the Edict of Potsdam and extended the exiles a welcome. Other electors followed suit and streams of refugees entered Germany.

For many of them, however, it proved to be only a temporary home. In the last part of the seventeenth century and the first part of the eighteenth there was a substantial dislocation of German population. In the period 1690-1777 over two hundred thousand emigrated to America. One impelling reason was the frequent changes of religions in the Palatinate after the Peace of Westphalia. This treaty afforded toleration to the Roman Catholic, Reformed, and Lutheran faiths, and permitted the prince of the territory to determine which one should be compulsory in his province. Under the territorial system dissidents had no alternative but to conform or leave. A second impelling reason for emigration was the invasion of the Palatinate in 1674, 1680, and 1688 by Louis XIV. Louis had spent a huge sum of money in an attempt to bribe the electors to choose him emperor of Germany, and when he failed he laid waste the land. A third reason was a devastating crop failure in 1708-1709 accompanied by such bitter cold that "the birds froze in the air and wild beasts in the forest."[10]

Unsuccessful attempts at settlement were made in Mississippi and in North Carolina. An epidemic of yellow fever in the former and an attack by the Indians in the latter liquidated the incipient colonies. Permanent settlements were made in New York, and especially in Pennsylvania when William Penn invited them to make that state their home. The first congregation was organized at Germantown in 1719, and there was urgent need for pastoral aid. In 1725 they asked John Philip Boehm, a capable young schoolteacher, to serve as their minister. In preaching and administering the sacraments he rendered competent and invaluable service. When an ordained minister arrived, George M. Weiss by name, the irregularity was pointedly obvious and advice in the matter was asked of the Dutch ministers in New York. They referred the matter to Classis Amsterdam, who gave the

10. Quoted by Dubbs, *German Reformed Church,* American Church History Series, VIII, p. 238.

wise advice that Boehm be ordained at once and that all of his past ministerial acts be judged "lawful" in view of the exceptional circumstances. He was ordained in 1729, and the intimate relations between the German Reformed and Classis Amsterdam continued until the German Reformed Church became independent in 1792. Scattered German Reformed churches were organized in Virginia and the Carolinas. In 1746 an excellent administrator, Michael Schlatter, took over the leadership. He established churches and schools, imported ministers, and arranged for the first synod, which met in Philadelphia in 1747. By 1794 the denomination had 178 churches and some 40,000 members. A century later it had increased its strength eightfold.

The fifth significant Calvinistic stream was the *Scotch-Irish,* whose strength was eventually concentrated in the Middle and Southern colonies.

The Scottish Reformation, which had its political overtones in that the Roman Catholics favored alliance with France while the Protestants desired political affiliation with England, was quite solidly established by 1557 when the Scottish nobles sympathetic to Protestantism formed the "Lords of the Congregation" and when in 1559 John Knox, the fearless and capable reformer, returned to give aggressive leadership. The Reformation spread into northeastern Ireland, notably the four counties of Ulster, when English and Scottish settlements were planted there by English rulers in an effort to extend their control over the island. These transplanted Calvinists proved to be excellent colonists and achieved a considerable measure of prosperity.

Despite their prosperous beginnings, they were not destined to remain there permanently. The English government began to levy economic restrictions in the form of Navigation Acts which curtailed their exports, and when, in addition, they were forced to pay tithes to the Irish Anglican Church, even though it was in the minority, they decided to leave for more congenial lands. By 1750, over one hundred thousand of them had emigrated to America.

The earliest Scotch-Irish immigrants, sensing their affinity to New England Calvinism, entered through the port of Boston and made initial settlements in the New England states.

It was soon evident, however, that the differences between them were not inconsiderable and after mounting tensions and after a series of disagreeable episodes the main body of the Scotch-Irish went southward into the Middle and Southern colonies, influencing the other establishments with their uniform and solid Presbyterianism.

The "Father of Presbyterianism" in America was Francis Makemie, consecrated Ulsterman who itinerated in Virginia, Maryland and the Carolinas in 1683. Despite active opposition by the Anglicans, who had virtually a state church in those states, he established churches, secured additional ministerial help from London, and by 1706 organized the first presbytery in Philadelphia, with six ministers in attendance. In 1716 the number of presbyteries had increased to four, the number of ministers to seventeen, most of whom came from Scotland, Ireland and New England, and the first synod was held. Although there was urgent need for more pastors, and the pressures were great for hasty ordination, the Presbyterians clung doggedly to their ideal of an educated ministry. In 1726 William Tennent, former priest in the Established Church of Ireland, inaugurated for the training of ministers Log College, the progenitor of Princeton. At the outbreak of the American Revolution the Presbyterian churches numbered five hundred.

As a consequence of this extensive immigration and internal growth it is estimated that of the total population of three million in this country in 1776 two-thirds of them were at least nominally Calvinistic. The judgment is warranted that "originally Calvinism dominated the American theological scene."[11]

Disintegration and Decay

Winfield Burggraaf, writing in 1928, asserted, "The first theology in American bore the unmistakable stamp of the person and teaching of John Calvin. The absolute sovereignty of God in all of human affairs was not only maintained theo-

11. C. Bouma, *Calvinism in Times of Crisis*, p. 77. At the outbreak of the Revolutionary War, the largest denominations were, in order: Congregationalists, Anglicans, Presbyterians, Baptists, Lutherans, German Reformed and Dutch Reformed. Roman Catholicism was tenth and Methodism twelfth in size.

retically . . . but was in reality the cornerstone upon which colonial statecraft as well as domestic life was based and upon which the stately structure of Puritan life was erected." But "today, three centuries later, the prevailing theology is far from Calvinistic."[12]

The seeds of decay were present very early. There were nonconformists and dissenters from the beginning. Within the first decade in New England two Anglicans as well as some Quakers, who placed the "inner light" above the Bible, were expelled from the colony. There was Ann Hutchinson, the antinomian, who confused the Biblical covenants, and denied the Calvinistic teachings of sanctification as an evidence of justification. She settled with her followers in Rhode Island. There was Roger Williams, who repudiated the covenant doctrine by his denial of the validity of infant baptism. He also found refuge in Rhode Island. There was William Pynchon, who wrote in 1650 *The Meritorious Price of Our Redemption* in which he rejected substitutionary atonement. There was the Half-way Covenant or Stoddardism, in which the covenant was violated in that children of non-confessing members were admitted to baptism, and the Lord's Supper was transformed into a converting ordinance. All of those facts were harbingers of defection and dissent that was to come.

It is worthy of note that the first defection reared its head in New England. And it did so for good reason. While the Dutch colony in New Amsterdam, for example, had its authoritative creed, in New England there was suspicion of humanly constructed creeds.[13] Moreover, New England had a greater number of original, creative theologians; it had closer contact with the liberal stream of thought of Europe"[14]; and it had autonomy of the local congregation, so that heresy could run an unimpeded course. But defection soon spread to the other colonies or arose within the other communions. *The Plan of Union* of 1801, for instance, in which Congregation-

12. Burggraaf, W. *The Rise and Development of Liberal Theology in America*, p. 1.

13. John Robinson, the first important leader of the Pilgrims, who remained in Holland but whose views were deeply engraven upon the Pilgrim colony, asserted that he wanted no creeds; all he was interested in was the Word of God.

14. *Ibid.*, p. 7.

alists and Presbyterians joined forces in supplying the spiritual needs of the frontier served to infect the latter body with the heresies present in the former.

The liberal theology that was eventually to engulf America assumed various forms, but all of them had the same basic root — the humanism of the Renaissance,[15] which was in turn a revival of the anthropocentricism of pagan antiquity. Humanism, as the term implies, is essentially man-centered and is thus the sworn enemy of theocentric Calvinism. On the American scene it takes the form of Arminianism, Universalism, Unitarianism, Classic Modernism, and Christian Realism.

Arminianism, which allows a measure of human contribution in the transaction of redemption and denies the five fundamental Calvinistic doctrines, spread to England through such agents as Hugo Grotius, jurist from Holland who lectured there; students and writers (e.g., John Locke) who spent some time in the Netherlands and on the continent; and through the spread of Arminian writings (the Cambridge Platonists, for instance, steeped themselves in the works of Episcopius). It had precipitated a crisis in Holland which led to the Synod of Dort (1618-1619). The Arminians were exiled, and thus their teachings were disseminated. By 1700 Arminianism had gathered many adherents in America and was spreading at an alarming rate. The Reforming Synod held in 1679 in New England when calamities were multitudinous was designed to counteract it, as was the Adopting Act of 1729 by which all ministers and licentiates in the Presbyterian church were forced to subscribe to the Westminster Confession and promise to uphold it. Jonathan Edwards, Sr. (1703-1758) put forth a valiant effort to stem that tide, preaching a series of sermons on justification by faith in 1743 to check Armini-

15. Burggraaf contends that the following elements in Erasmus's teachings are perceptible throughout liberal theology: "(a) permits religious tolerance within the same church group; (b) makes religion to consist of ethics: cultural training rather than regeneration, not grace but the *bonae literae;* (c) Christ is the teacher, the 'heavenly doctor', (d) the heart of Christianity is to be found in the Ten Commandments, the Sermon on the Mount and the Lord's Prayer; (e) the God of the Jews is not the God of the Christians; (f) man has free will, for the command to do involves ability to do . . .; (g) intense aversion to dogma." *Ibid.,* pp. 42-43.

anism. That series touched off the Great Awakening, the first great revival in America. By his herculaean efforts "the elimination of Calvinism as a determining factor in New England, which seemd to be immanent as he wrote, was postponed for a hundred years."[16]

Calvinism fared ill, however, with the successors of the senior Edwards. The younger Edwards (1745-1801) broke with Calvinism on the atonement when he accepted the governmental view of Grotius, in which the emphasis is shifted from God as sovereign to God as moral governor of the universe and when, in distinction from his father, who taught "moral inability and natural inability," he taught, as did Joseph Bellamy (1719-1790), "moral inability but natural ability." Nathaniel Taylor (1781-1858), taught that God was limited, grace was resistible, and sin consisted only in voluntary acts, and Samuel Hopkins (1721-1803), with others, taught general atonement. The breakdown of New England theology meant the breakdown of Calvinism.

The major revivals after the Great Awakening were designed to reclaim the thousands who had pushed across the frontier in the westward trek and had failed to keep their church membership vital. This negligence, along with the floods of infidelity that reached America after the Revolutionary War, made America a fertile mission field. The denominations most active in frontier evangelism were the Methodists, the Baptists, and the Presbyterian Reactionaries, all of whom were impelled by an Arminian theology, since that appeared to comport best with the rising democratic spirit of the West.[17]

16. J. Hastings, ed., *Encyclopedia of Religion and Ethics,* Vol. V., p. 226. Estimates vary as to the strict Calvinism of Jonathan Edwards, Sr. Shelton Smith, Borden, P. Y. De Jong, *et al.,* contend that he taught imputation, but Warfield, Gerstner, *et al.,* disagree. Burggraaf says that he subjectified the inner testimony of the Holy Spirit, but Gerstner interprets him differently. Twenty-seven publications of Edwards are extant, including his trenchant criticism of Arminian anthropology entitled *Freedom of the Will.* A completely new edition of the works of Jonathan Edwards is in the process of being published by the Yale University Press. The first volume, *Freedom of the Will,* edited by Paul Ramsey, appeared in 1957.

17. "Through the spirit of Revivalism the emphasis in theology shifted from Calvinistic objectivism to American subjectivism, from Calvinistic theocentricity to American anthropocentricity, from Calvinistic theocratic collectivism to American democratic individualism." Hammar, *op. cit.,* p. 83.

In the second Awakening in 1800 there was, for example, a Barton W. Stone, "who at his ordination had stated that he received the Westminster Confession only so far as it was consistent with the Word of God, and others . . . who preached that God loved the whole world, that Jesus died for all men, and that sinners were able to accept the means of Salvation."[18] Out of that revival sprang the Cumberland Presbyterian Church, which revised its Westminster Confession in the direction of universal atonement and repudiation of the doctrine of infant damnation. The Revival of 1857 was marked in the main by extensive prayer meetings, but the other nineteenth century revivals, sparked by Charles E. Finney, who was "inclined to be unsparing in his criticism of the Calvinistic theology,"[19] definitely tended to assume a free will in man. The later revivals led by Moody and Billy Sunday went in the same direction, so that Arminianism became firmly entrenched and evangelicalism in America today is predominately Arminian in theology.

Liberalism took the form secondly of Universalism, which had its greatest appeal in small towns and rural areas.

The Arminian position that Christ has earned salvation for all men and God has made provision for man so that all can accept, found further development in the revival of the position that all men will eventually be saved, a heresy that appeared at least as early as the time of Origen (c.185-c.254). Jonathan Mayhew, an anti-Trinitarian, criticized the doctrine of reprobation vigorously in 1762. In 1770 there came to America a convert of George Whitefield who was destined to become the minister of the first Universalist Church in America. He was John Murray, a vigorous reactionary against the doctrine of eternal punishment in Calvinism, who settled in Gloucester, Massachusetts, and began the Universalist Church there in 1779. In 1782 Charles Chaucy wrote *The Salvation of All Men, Illustrated and Vindicated as a Scripture Doctrine,* calling the doctrines of election and reprobation "horrible absurdities" and asserting that there was no "partial design . . . and effect of the mediating inter-position of Jesus Christ."[20] The

18. F. G. Beardsley, *The History of Christianity in America,* p. 103.
19. *Ibid.,* pp. 139-140.
20. Quoted by Burggraaf, *op. cit.,* pp. 59-60.

most influential Universalist theologian was Hosea Ballou (1771-1852), son of a Calvinistic Baptist preacher. Ballou was converted to the Universalist position by his study of Romans 5:12. The rationalistic impact of Ethan Allen's *Reason the Only Oracle of Man* led him to repudiate the doctrines of the Trinity, the deity of Christ, and substitutionary atonement. The younger Edwards made able reply to Universalist propositions, and although churches were ultimately established all over the country the movement never gained appreciable strength.

Much greater strength was evident in the third form which theological liberalism took, Unitarianism. This belief had more appeal for the intelligentsia and captured the bulk of churches in New England.

The Great Awakening, in which Jonathan Edwards, Sr., and George Whitefield, both of whom emphasized human depravity and salvation by grace, played the most significant roles, precipitated considerable doctrinal discussion. In this discussion Unitarian ideas began to emerge. Among the first to enunciate them was Jonathan Mayhew, the liberal preacher of Boston,[21] who claimed that "total depravity is both dishonorable to the character of God and a libel on human nature."[22] Unitarianism was not, as might be supposed, "in the first place a reaction against the doctrine of the Trinity . . . . It was a revolt against the prevalent Calvinistic doctrines of total depravity, substitutionary and limited atonement."[23] Its two foci, both of which come into sharp perspective in later liberalism, were: faith in human goodness and confidence in human reason.[24] Organizationally it dates its rise in 1787 when James Freeman was ordained by the church wardens of King's Chapel in Boston. Two years previously, that church had voted to omit from its order of worship all references to the Trinity. The appointment of Henry Ware, an avowed Unitarian, to a professorship

21. See above, p. 125.
22. R. G. Wilburn, *The Prophetic Voice in American Christianity*, p. 50.
23. Burggraaf, *op. cit.*, p. 59.
24. Note the radical departure from John Robinson the Separatist, who maintained that "divine authority is to sway with us above all reason; yet reason teacheth, that God is both to be believed and obeyed in the things for which man can see no reason." Quoted by Burggraaf, *op. cit.*, p. 10.

of divinity at Harvard in 1805[25], served to sharpen the rising cleavage within the Congregational churches. The turning point occurred in 1819 when William Ellery Channing delivered his "Baltimore Sermon" at the ordination of Jared Sparks. After that event 120 churches went over to Unitarianism. The American Unitarian Association was formed in 1825. Although Channing retained some vestiges of conservatism, saying that Christ was more than a mere man and that the Bible was in some sense authoritative, to all practical purposes he elevated human reason above the Scriptures. He said of total depravity that "a more irrational doctrine could not be contrived" and "were it really believed . . . men would look up with dread and detestation to the author of their being, and look round with horror on their fellow-creatures."[26] Unitarian ideas were publicized and propagated by Ralph Waldo Emerson, one time preacher, Transcendentalist poet and philosopher, who substituted religious intuition for supernatural revelation and maintained that Christianity was diseased with the "mumps and measles" of the doctrines of original sin, depravity and predestination.[27] The extreme radicalism of Theodore Parker, thoroughly imbued as he was with Deism and German Biblical Criticism, meant a split into Conservative and Radical Unitarianism, the former finding continuance and kinship in later liberalism and the latter issuing into bald naturalism. By 1825, 80 percent of the Congregational churches in New England had gone Unitarian.

Liberalism also took the form of "The New Divinity" or Classic Modernism. Walter Marshal Horton has called the period of 1850-1914 "the great age of liberalism in America." Then it was that the older liberalism was colored and "enriched" by new elements, and "The New Divinity" is the result of this attempt "to take up and neutralize the shock brought about by the sudden rise of the natural sciences and the influx from Germany of the rationalistic-critical theology."[28] The optimistic view of man which had resulted from the denial

25. Andover Seminary was started in 1808 in protest, but it also capitulated to Unitarianism in due time.
26. Wilburn, *op. cit.*, p. 51.
27. *Ibid.*
28. Burggraaf, *op. cit.*, p. 160.

of the doctrines of total depravity and original sin was further promoted by the Darwinian theory of evolution. At first the theologians were hostile to or suspicious of it, but led by H. W. Beecher, Washington Gladden and others, many of them gradually capitulated and agreed with Lyman Abbott that "God has but one way of doing this . . . the way of growth, of development, of evolution."[29] The motif of progress was applied to history by the German Albrecht Ritschl, in his reinterpretation of the Biblical concept of the Kingdom of God.[30] That Kingdom was not to be construed as eschatological, finding its full realization in the next world, nor simply as a commonwealth of born-again Christians, but as "an association of men for reciprocal and common action from the motive of love."[31] By improvement of living conditions and relationships between men, by elevating the standard of living, and by ameliorating the ills of society, the Kingdom of God would gradually be realized on earth. That reinterpretation worked "hand-in-glove" with the rise of the Social Gospel, another feature of the New Divinity. Christianity was not to be viewed as primarily individualistic, providing salvation for the sinner who had violated the laws of God and offended His holiness, but social, removing the injustices and inequities among men and excising the evils from society. There was little patience with creeds and propositional truth, for "Christianity is not a doctrine, but a life." Washington Gladden and Walter Rauschenbusch sought to provide a theology for this activistic Christianity and located it in the universal Fatherhood of God (whose main attribute is love), the universal brotherhood of man, and in a human Jesus who "saves" men by teaching them to be like God.

The immanence of God, to the virtual exclusion of His transcendence, became the reigning principle of the new theology. The emphasis was upon continuity between revelation and natural religion, Christianity and other religions, God and man, and Christ and mankind. Horton has written: "In liberal

29. Quoted by H. S. Coffin, *Religion Yesterday and Today,* p. 9.

30. From Bushnell on there is the reading of new meanings into the old theological terms by American theologians. Bushnell also taught the *Moral Influence* theory of the atonement.

31. A. Ritschl, *The Christian Doctrine of Justification and Reconciliation,* p. 210.

Protestant thought the old clear-cut distinction between reason and revelation has been abolished, because human discovery and divine disclosures have come to be regarded as two sides of the same process."[32]

The writings of Ritschl, noted above, as well as those of Schleiermacher, who reduced religion to a "sense of dependence on God" and emphasized the subjective, and Immanuel Kant, who virtually equated religion with morality, were influential in American theology. So too were direct contacts with German thought. A considerable number of American students pursued study in Germany in the latter half of the nineteenth century, and they took back with them many radical theological ideas, including the Higher Criticism of the Bible. A cardinal feature of the New Divinity, Higher or Historical Criticism meant the repudiation of a "biased" standpoint. That is the Bible must not be approached as the divinely inspired and infallible Word of God, but it must be analyzed and judged as any other book. Thus, the Bible lost its authoritative character, and it came to be viewed as a record of man's religious experiences arrived at by empiricism, or the "scientific method," rather than God's redemptive disclosure to men.

By 1913 The New Divinity had engulfed the American church world and Washington Gladden could write, "The idea of the immanence of God; the idea that God's method of working is the method of evolution; the idea that nature in all its deepest meanings is supernatural; the idea of the constant presence of God in our lives; the idea of the universal divine Fatherhood and of the universal human Brotherhood . . . those are ideas which are here to stay."[33]

He was only partially right. The first World War dealt a severe blow to classic modernism and there resulted Christian Realism, or what might be called chastened Modernism. The optimism of the old modernism with its doctrines of inevitable progress and human perfectibility was rudely shattered by the outbreak of a conflict of global proportions. And when it was followed by a staggering depression, The New Divinity was forced to take inventory. From it there emerged a sobering or chastened liberalism. As Kerschner remarked, "World

32. W. M. Horton, *Revelation,* p. 242.
33. W. Gladden, *Present Day Theology,* pp. 6-7.

events served to brush aside trivialities and surface optimisms and to reveal the necessity for grounding one's faith upon a profounder basis."[34] A series of autobiographical articles in the *Christian Century* in the 30s on the subject "How My Mind Has Changed in the Last Decade" reflects that reassessment. Various remedies were proposed: a shift from ethics to religion, a return to the writings of St. Paul, and elimination of "romantic illusions." "Back to the facts then, back to all the facts, back to the grim facts of the actual world, and back to sound thinking on those facts, the liberal theology must go."[35]

Specifically, a chastened modernism sounds the call, firstly, for a more realistic anthropology. The vast majority of its proponents concede that man has been regarded altogether too optimistically. Walter Marshal Horton says he has restored "original sin" to his theology, Harry Emerson Fosdick warns against reading the reality out of sin, and W. L. Sperry calls for a "realistic and credible doctrine of man."[36] Accompanying this more realistic anthropology is a measure of skepticism with respect to modern social programs and panaceas. Certain it is that the trend of contemporary events "has served to reinforce in American Protestantism the notion that evil cannot be disregarded or even treated as lightly as the followers of Albrecht Ritschl and their descendants were accustomed to do."[37]

Secondly, there is recognition of the need of reconstruction of the idea of God. Fosdick holds that the old liberalism relegated God to an advisory role and "watered down and thinned out the central message and distinctive truth of religion, the reality of God."[38] Foster calls for a return to the neglected truths of the sternness and justice of God, and men like Wieman and Bennett decry the extreme emphasis on the immanence of God and call for a new appreciation of His transcendence and "otherness." There is recognition of the

34. F. D. Kerschner, "Realities and Vision," *Christian Century*, LVI (1939), p. 149.

35. F. H. Foster, *The Modern Movement in Theology*, p. 214.

36. W. L. Sperry, "How My Mind Has Changed," *Christian Century*, LVI (1939), p. 187.

37. P. Woolley, "American Calvinism in the 20th Century" in *American Calvinism*, p. 52.

38. H. E. Fosdick, "Beyond Modernism," *Christian Century*, LVI (1939), p. 1551.

fact that religion has been virtually reduced to humanism. "Man today is not satisfied with self-culture and with the echo of his own voice, sent back as the only answer from the infinite mystery'."[39]

Thirdly, chastened liberalism acknowledges that although Christ has been honored in a measure, He has not received His full due. We need to pay more attention to His cross and resurrection, says Georgia Harkness, and see much more in Him than a great martyr dying for His convictions.[40]

Such is the judgment of at least a segment of modern religious liberalism as it sits in judgment upon itself. It is by no means ready to return to the position of historic orthodoxy and it has serious strictures with respect to Barthianism, but by adopting a more realistic attitude it hopes by its own genius and method to resolve the spiritual and religious problems of mankind.

Preservation and Perpetuation of Calvinism

As we have already observed, the New England stream of Calvinism was early muddied by Arminianism and other forms of liberalism. Some attempt to stem the tide or purify the stream was made by the Ministerial Associations proposed by the Mathers,[41] and by the valiant efforts of Jonathan Edwards, Sr. But Congregationalism gradually succumbed, leaving individual Calvinists and struggling evangelical groups in New England. The German Reformed Church, which was progressively infiltrated with contrary winds of doctrine, also declined.

The Reformed Church of America (Dutch Reformed Church) held the Calvinistic line until the opening of the ninenteenth century. Then the rise of Hopkinsianism and Arminianism within its ranks occasioned in 1822 a secession led by the Rev. Solomon Froeligh which brought about the True Reformed Dutch Church. This church aimed to continue the Calvinistic tradition. There were divisive tendencies in the seceding group, and a segment of this church

39. Sperry, *op. cit.,* p. 187.
40. G. Harkness, "A Spiritual Pilgrimage," *Christian Century* LVI (1939), p. 348.
41. See above, p. 115.

united with the Christian Reformed Church in 1877. The French Huguenots were absorbed into other communions.

The Scotch-Irish stream deposited Presbyterianism on American soil. It, too, was threatened by divergent doctrines, and in the Adopting Act of 1729 it demanded of all ministers and licentiates subscription to the Westminster Confession in order that the threat of Arminianism be warded off. The spread of liberalism through the Plan of Union merger of Congregationalists and Presbyterians in their missionary program led to a cleavage in 1836 between the Old School (conservative) and New School (liberal) Presbyterians. Reunion between those two groups was effected in 1869. Princeton Seminary, which was founded in 1812, carried on the Old School tradition and promoted conservatism under the Hodges and under B. B. Warfield. Warfield dominated the scene in his tenure of thirty-four years (1887 to 1921). But the pressure for a liberalized, inclusivistic theology grew apace. Heresy trials involving Briggs, Smith, and McGiffert marked the closing decade of the nineteenth century. The Westminster Confession was subjected to a liberalizing revision in 1903; in 1906 reunion with the Arminianistic Cumberland Presbyterian Church was affected; and in 1924 some 1274 ministers of the Presbyterian Church signed the Auburn Affirmation. This document advocated tolerance and flexibility of interpretation of five basic, historic Christian doctrines. The rift between conservatives and liberals steadily widened. In 1929 Westminster Seminary was established as a protest institution and it was followed shortly by the formation of the Orthodox Presbyterian Church.

Calvinism in America today is a "struggling remnant." There are, to be sure, individual Calvinists and groups of Calvinists in the evangelical denominations, but organizationally there are only five or six small denominations that are still quite thoroughly imbued with Calvinism. They include the Christian Reformed Church, which is rooted in a secession from the State Church of the Netherlands, and which dates its origin in 1857, subscribes to the Belgic Confession, Heidelberg Catechism and Canons of Dort, and numbers (according to the 1957 census) 481 churches and 204,621 members in the United States and Canada; the Orthodox Presbyterian

Church, which has the Westminster Confession and the Westminster Shorter and Longer Catechisms as symbols and numbers 83 churches and 8754 members; the Protestant Reformed Church and its offshoot the Orthodox Protestant Reformed Church, each of which has about 18 churches and 2500 members and both of whom subscribe to the Belgic Confession, the Heidelberg Catechism and the Canons of Dort; the Reformed Presbyterian Church of North America, which originated in Scotland during the seventeenth century in protest against the king's attempt to make the Church of Scotland episcopal, and which subscribes to the Westminster Confession and numbers 74 churches and 6442 members; the Associate Reformed Presbyterian Church, Scottish Covenanter in lineage, the issue of an eighteenth-century secession in which Erskine was the key figure, now concentrated in South Carolina, operating Erskine College and having 147 ministers, 151 churches, and 27,000 members; and possibly the Free Magyar Reformed Church, which originated in Hungary, began in America in 1904, and which now numbers 27 churches and 9000 members and uses as its doctrinal standards the Second Helvetic Confession and the Heidelberg Catechism.

BIBLIOGRAPHY

Bacon, Leonard C., *A History of American Christianity,* American Church History Series XIII, New York, 1930.

Baird, C. W., *The Huguenot Emigration to America,* 2 vols., New York, 1879.

Beardsley, F. G., *The History of Christianity in America,* New York, 1938.

Bouma, Clarence (ed.), *Calvinism in Times of Crisis,* Grand Rapids, 1947.

Brauer, Jerald, *Protestantism in America,* Philadelphia, 1953.

Burggraaf, Winfield, *The Rise and Development of Liberal Theology in America,* Amsterdam, 1928.

Corwin, E. T., *The Dutch Reformed Church,* American Church History Series, VIII, New York, 1895.

Dubbs, J. H., *The German Reformed Church,* American Church History Series, VIII, New York, 1895.

Foster, F. H., *The Modern Movement in Theology,* New York, 1939.

Gillett, E. H., *History of the Presbyterian Church in the U.S.A.,* Philadelphia, 1864.

Hammar, George, *Christian Realism in Contemporary, American Theology,* Upsala, Sweden, 1940.

Hoogstra, Jacob T. (ed.), *American Calvinism,* Grand Rapids, 1957.

Johnson, T. C., *A History of the Presbyterian Church in the U. S.,* American Church History Series, II, New York, 1894.

Loetscher, Lefferts A., *The Broadening Church,* Philadelphia, 1954.

McNeill, John T., *The History and Character of Calvinism,* New York, 1954.

Miller, Perry, *The New England Mind,* New York, 1939.

Sweet, William W., *The Story of Religions in America,* New York, 1930.

Wilburn, R. G., *The Prophetic Voice in Protestant Christianity,* St. Louis, 1956.